the Teen Body BOOK

A YOUR BODY, YOURSELF BOOK

the Teen Body Book

a guide to your changing body

by Judie Lewellen

illustrated by Mary Bryson, M.A.M.S., and Wendy Wahman

LOWELL HOUSE JUVENILE

LOS ANGELES

NTC/Contemporary Publishing Group

To my patient husband, Michael Parrish

Published by Lowell House
A division of NTC/Contemporary Publishing Group, Inc.
4255 West Touhy Avenue, Lincolnwood (Chicago), Illinois 60712 U.S.A.

Managing Director and Publisher: Jack Artenstein
Director of Publishing Services: Rena Copperman
Editorial Director: Brenda Pope-Ostrow
Project Editor: Dianne J. Woo
Typesetting & Design: Carolyn Wendt

Lowell House books can be purchased at special discounts
when ordered in bulk for premiums and special sales.
Contact Customer Service at the address above, or call 1-800-323-4900.

Printed and bound in the United States of America

Library of Congress Catalog Card Number: 99-73107

ISBN: 0-7373-0165-1

DHD 10 9 8 7 6 5 4 3

CONTENTS

The Teen Body Book will clear up a lot of questions you have about your feelings and about growing up. However, no book can answer every question you might have as you enter your teen years. If you have a question you need answered, don't be afraid to talk to an adult about it—especially your mom or dad! You may even want to sit down with a parent and read through parts of this book together.

This book is not intended to treat, diagnose, or prescribe. For any physical problems you think you may have, talk to your doctor. If you feel you may have a serious emotional problem, consult a licensed psychological counselor.

The Time of Your Life

If you're a teenager or almost a teen, you've probably noticed that something is happening to your body. You still feel like the same you, but your body is frantically waving a big red flag that is signaling that something is definitely up: "Construction ahead. Prepare to slow down, speed up, or go a little crazy at times."

Something *is* up. Your body is going through puberty. It's the time in your life when your body starts to change from that of a child to that of an adult. It's a time when your sex organs develop and mature. You are now an adolescent—an in-betweener—no longer a child, but not yet an adult. You may feel marooned on a bridge between two worlds, and this can no doubt be strange and confusing.

The Teen Body Book is your road map. It explains what's taking place inside your body and mind and helps you cross that bridge to adulthood. Above all, it's meant to reassure you that you're OK—in other words, refreshingly normal—and to answer your questions.

You'll learn how girls and guys develop physically, sexually, and emotionally. The discussions of girls and guys are organized into two separate chapters. Read both of them. The more you know about the opposite sex, the better equipped you'll be to understand them and develop lasting relationships.

Even if you've talked with your friends or parents about sex, you most likely have questions that haven't been answered. Chapter 5 is filled with information so that you can find out everything you should know but are afraid to ask.

Are you going through more ups and downs than an elevator? Do you sometimes feel things couldn't get any better, and the next minute you think they couldn't get any worse? Check out the chapter on dealing with your changing emotions. You'll find out what to do when you get the blues, how to manage your anger, and how to cope with stress.

In addition, we've included chapters on nutrition, exercise, and health concerns common among all teens—acne, hair growth, body odor. We also address your concerns about infectious diseases and how to avoid falling into the trap of tobacco, alcohol, and drugs.

You have the power to make these years among the best in your life by getting to know your body, feeling comfortable in it, and learning to maintain this remarkable piece of human machinery. So get psyched, get physical, get cracking. Your whole future is ahead of you!

$\mathcal{B}$ody Talk

Every time my mom's friends come over, they stare at me and say something like, "Oh, you're not a little kid anymore," or "Well, you're certainly growing up. Are those whiskers?" It makes me feel weird and embarrassed so I just go to my room. My mom says I'm being rude, but I don't think I am.

—Sean, age 14

$\mathcal{Y}$ou know the feeling. Someone makes a comment about your body, and you just want to crawl into a hole and pull it in after you. It doesn't even have to be a negative comment. How many times do you need to hear Grandma say you used to be "this high"? Doesn't she think you've heard it a thousand times before?

And if your mom or dad asks you about it later, you really can't explain why you think the way you do. It's just that Grandma makes you feel even more awkward about something you're already feeling awkward enough about: your body.

Just what *is* happening to your body? More than that, what's happening to *you*?

You've no doubt noticed that your body is changing. You feel the same yet...different. Your body seems to be telling you that something is going on. Something is: you're going through a period of growth that is affecting the way you feel, the way you think, and the way you look.

But you're no stranger to change. Your body has already gone through a lot of it. Dig out those family photo albums—you know, the ones that make you cringe every time your mom pulls them out to show to Aunt Marge—and check out the pictures of you as a chubby baby. Then turn a few pages and there you are again, only this time you're probably 4 years old, you've lost your baby fat, and you've grown about 2 feet.

Now your body is going through another phase. It's called *puberty*. You are changing from a child into a sexually mature adult. That's why your feelings, both physical and emotional, can vary from one day to the next.

Puberty can begin at any age. Some guys enter puberty at around 9 years of age, while others start to mature at 12 or older. For some girls, it starts around age 8; for others, it begins at age 11 or older. The average age is 10½. No one can explain why one person may start at 9 and another at 13. Whatever time *you* begin is perfectly normal for *you*.

During puberty, your sex organs—both inside and outside your body—begin to grow and develop. Your body begins to change shape, and you start to notice hair where you never had any before. Your sexual development takes place gradually, over the course of five stages. The first stage actually begins when you are born and continues throughout your childhood years, to about age 8 or 9 or whenever you enter puberty, the second stage.

Scientists don't know *why* puberty happens or what triggers it, but they know *how* it happens. Stage 2 actually begins inside your brain. The part of the brain called the *hypothalamus* secretes a chemical, gonadotropin-releasing hormone (GnRH). This hormone causes the *pituitary,* a gland deep in the brain, to produce luteinizing hormone (LH) and follicle-stimulating hormone (FSH). LH and FSH then travel to the *gonads,* or sex organs—the *testicles* in guys and the *ovaries* in girls. These hormones "turn on" the testicles and ovaries, causing them to produce special hormones that tell your reproductive organs to grow and mature.

You don't need to memorize all these terms; it's more important that you have a general idea of what's behind the changes your body is going through. We describe the changes that happen to girls in the next chapter, then move on to what happens to guys in chapter 3. In chapter 4, we talk about what happens to everyone's body.

erstory

In gym class, we have to wear uniforms and take show-
ers. I feel nervous about undressing and being naked
in front of everyone, even if they're all girls. I know I
shouldn't be ashamed of my body, but I can't help it.
How long am I going to feel this way?

—Cassie, age 12

If you're like most girls, you want to know what's going on inside your body—
and your head. You may have just bought this cool new swimsuit, but you feel
self-conscious about wearing it around other people, even your friends. Or you're
looking forward to the slumber party this weekend, but you're nervous about getting undressed in front of everyone, and you're worried that you're going to look
like a geek in your pajamas or nightgown or sleep shirt.

Relax. Most, if not all, of the other girls feel the exact same way you do—only
they're not saying. If one of your friends confided these feelings to you, you'd
probably tell her not to worry about it, and that she'll look great, and who cares
what the others will think. So why not listen to your own advice?

Can't Hardly Wait

This period in your life can be both exciting and scary. Exciting because every experience is new and different, and scary because you don't know what to expect because, well, everything is new and different. You can't wait to grow up, yet at the same time you wish you could stay a kid forever.

Knowing what is happening to your body can help you get a handle on your feelings. In a nutshell, this is what's going to change: your breasts will increase in size, your vulva (what are referred to as your private parts) will

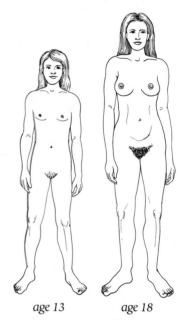

age 13   age 18

enlarge and develop, and your reproductive organs inside your body will undergo many, many changes in preparation for you to make and support a baby, even though you probably do not plan on having children for 15 or 20 years. The above illustration shows the average girl's body at two different ages.

You'll probably find questions you've been wanting to ask in the list below. Lots of girls have asked the very same questions you have, so you're not alone. They're answered in the text that follows.

✿ All of a sudden I'm growing like crazy. I'm about a foot taller than almost everyone—even the guys—in my class! Is this normal?

✿ One of my breasts is bigger than the other. Am I going to look lopsided for the rest of my life?

✿ When should I start doing breast self-examinations, and how do I do them?

✿ What are the correct names for my private parts? I don't want to sound like a little kid when I talk about them.

✿ My best friend got her first period a year and a half ago, and I still haven't gotten mine. We're the same age. Is something wrong with me?

✿ I got my first period when I was 13, but then I didn't have another one for four months. Why aren't they coming each month?

✿ Should I use sanitary napkins or tampons? I've heard you can get a disease from using tampons.

✿ Sometimes my underpants have wet stains on them. What are they?

The Air Up There

During puberty, your body becomes more curvy: your legs, thighs, hips, and buttocks grow rounder. Your breasts start to develop. Some girls develop more curves than others, and some "stretch out" more than others. Everyone develops differently. Even if your body looks somewhat like it did during childhood, you're still normal.

At the start of puberty, girls sometimes go through what's called a growth spurt, a period of rapid growth, which is why they may find themselves not only taller than other girls their age, but also taller than the guys. If this happens to you, don't fret too much about it. Again, it's normal. You'll slow down eventually, or the others will catch up to you. It all evens out in the end. Besides, basketball jokes aside, being able to do things some guys can't is something to take pride in.

Keeping Abreast

Like most girls, you're probably curious about when your breasts will begin to develop. Some girls start at 8 or 9 years old, while others don't begin until they are 15. Each girl's body has its own "clock" that tells it when to enter a new growth phase.

The illustrations below show the five stages of breast development. Your breasts won't "pop out" all at once. It's a gradual process, and takes about four or five years for your breasts to reach their mature adult size.

Stage 1 shows a girl in the pre-puberty stage. The breasts are flat except for the nipples.

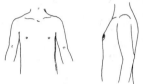

Stage 1

In **stage 2**, when puberty begins, the tissue of the breast begins growing. Breast buds, slightly raised areas, form. The nipples start to enlarge. The areola, the circle of skin surrounding each nipple, gets wider and darker.

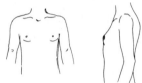

Stage 2

During **stage 3**, the breasts and areolas continue to grow larger.

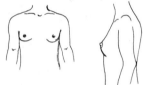

Stage 3

Stage 4 shows the nipple and areola forming a mound that sticks out slightly from the rest of the breast.

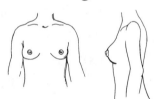

Stage 4

At the end of **stage 5**, the breasts are round and full. The nipples stick out and may point upward slightly. The areola is no longer a raised mound.

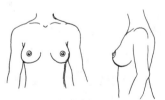

Stage 5

Not all girls' breasts go through all five stages. Many girls skip a stage. You may go from stage 2 to stage 4 and totally bypass stage 3. Also, not all women will have breasts like those pictured in stage 5. Most girls start their periods during stage 3 or 4.

Remember, however, that these are general descriptions. Just because your friend is already wearing a bra and you feel like you couldn't even fill an egg cup yet, doesn't mean something is wrong with you. And your breasts will change in size during various times throughout your life: menstruation, pregnancy, and after *menopause* (when your ovaries stop releasing eggs and you stop having periods; this usually occurs after age 45).

Don't be alarmed if one of your breasts is larger than the other. It's totally normal—and not noticeable by anyone but you! Despite what you think you see in magazines and on television, Beverly Peele and all those other supermodels don't have "perfect," mirror-image breasts—at least, not if they're the breasts they were born with. Take a look in the mirror. You'll see that the right side of your face isn't exactly like the left side. And like most people, one of your arms may even be slightly longer than the other. So you're not alone.

ANATOMY OF A BREAST

The breast contains 15 to 20 sections, called *lobes,* each of which is surrounded by fat. This fatty tissue, supported by connective tissue, is what helps give breasts their shape. The rest of the breast is made up of nerves, arteries, and lymph channels, but no muscle.

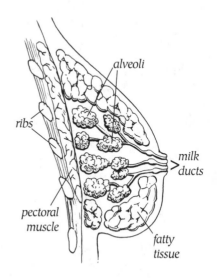

Inside each lobe are glands called *alveoli.* When a woman has a baby, the alveoli produce milk, or *lactate.* The milk travels down ducts that end at the nipple. The skin of the areola surrounding the nipple is thin and contains sweat and oil glands as well as hair follicles, so it's not unusual for a few strands to grow around your nipples.

Cross Section of a Breast

Your milk ducts and fatty tissue begin to develop when you enter puberty. These ducts and fat are what form your breast buds.

BREAST SELF-EXAMINATION

Examining your breasts on a regular basis is a must. The earlier any lump or abnormality is found, the more effective treatment may be. A good time to do a self-exam is about a week after your period ends, when your breasts aren't as sensitive. Even if you haven't had a period yet, it's a good idea to start this practice now so you get into the habit.

During the self-exam, look and feel for any lumps or thickening of tissue. By doing this every month, you will become familiar with your breasts and will notice any changes. Most irregularities you find at your age are *not* cancerous. If you do notice something, though, see your doctor just to be safe.

The examination has two parts: a visual exam and a manual exam.

> ### JUST SWELL
>
> The human breast is unlike any other in the animal kingdom. In female apes and monkeys, the breasts swell only when the female needs to nurse her young. After the baby is weaned, the ape's breasts flatten back down. In humans, the breasts swell during puberty—before the first pregnancy even occurs—and remain that way throughout life.

Eye Spy: Visual Exam

1. Stand in front of a mirror under a bright light. Carefully inspect each breast by looking in the mirror and checking for any bulges, depressions, swelling, or changes in color.

2. Examine your nipples. If they normally stick out, have they become inverted? Have the areolas changed color, or do they feel different?

3. Place both your hands behind your head. Scan your breasts again. Then put your hands on your hips and

look again. Lumps sometimes show up only when you have your hands in one of these positions.

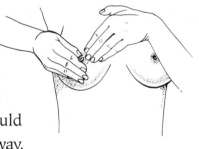

4. Give each nipple a gentle squeeze. Any fluid, clear or milky, that appears is not necessarily a sign that something is wrong, but you should schedule an appointment with your doctor anyway.

Give Yourself a Hand: Manual Exam

You can perform this part either in the shower or tub, or lying down.

In the Shower or Tub

1. Your hand will glide more easily over your breasts if they are wet and soapy. Keeping the fingers of your right hand flat, place your hand on your left breast. Raise your left arm over your head to stretch out the breast tissue.

2. Pressing down firmly, make small circular motions with the fingers of your right hand. Begin at your nipple and work your way outward, making your circles larger and larger, until you have covered the entire breast. Be sure to run your fingers over your armpit and up to your shoulder; there is breast tissue in these areas, too.

3. Repeat steps 1 and 2, this time with your left hand and right breast. Remember to lift your right arm over your head.

Lying Down

1. Place a small pillow under your left shoulder.

2. Tuck your left hand under your head, elbow bent. Keeping the fingers of your right hand flat, press down firmly on your left breast, making small circular motions starting at the nipple. Continue working outward until the entire breast has been covered. Don't forget to press your fingers under your armpit and up to your shoulder.

3. Move the pillow to your right shoulder and repeat the exam with your right breast.

Say It Right

Since you're on your way to becoming an adult, you'll feel a lot cooler talking about your body if you know the correct name for the part you're describing. You may hear girls referring to the area between their legs as their "vagina" when, in fact, it is actually called the *vulva,* or the genital organs that lie outside the body. The illustration at right details the various parts of the vulva.

The best way to become familiar—and comfortable—with your body is to use a hand mirror to look at yourself. If you haven't done this before, it's OK to feel a little reluctant or even ashamed. Once you try it, though, you'll see how easy it is, not to mention interesting!

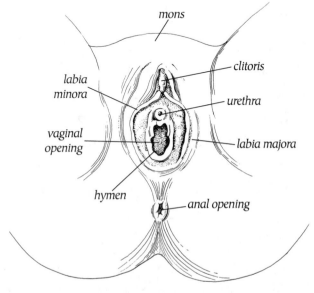

External Female Genitalia

Here's the vocabulary you'll need so you won't have to rely on slang terms.

The mons

The mons is the pad of fat that lies right under the skin covering your pubic bone. *Mons* is the Latin word for "little hill." You can see it if you stand sideways in front of a large mirror. The mons grows thicker and higher as you mature. The appearance of pubic hair on the mons is a sign that you have entered puberty.

The labia majora

The vulva divides into two folds of skin, or *labia,* which protect the openings to your vagina and urethra. The outer folds are called the *labia majora,* or outer lips. In Latin, *labia* means "lips" and *majora* means "large." During puberty, hair begins to grow on the labia majora, as it does on the mons.

The labia minora

These are the inner lips, or folds of skin, under the labia majora. If you use your hand to part your outer lips, you can see the inner lips on either side of your vaginal opening. The labia minora are smaller (*minora* means "small") and hairless but contain oil and sweat glands.

The clitoris

The clitoris is the nub of flesh located just below the point where the labia minora come together to form a hood, right beneath the mons. The clitoris grows larger during puberty. Packed with blood vessels and nerve endings that send messages to the pleasure center of the brain, the clitoris is sensitive to touch and can cause sexual arousal in a woman. Once stimulated, it swells and becomes even more sensitive.

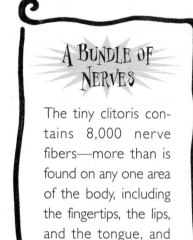

A BUNDLE OF NERVES

The tiny clitoris contains 8,000 nerve fibers—more than is found on any one area of the body, including the fingertips, the lips, and the tongue, and twice the number found in the penis.

The urethra

The opening and the tube itself from which urine flows out of the body is called the urethra. It is found beneath the clitoris and above the vaginal opening.

The vaginal opening

This is the opening beneath the urethra that leads to the vagina; it connects your outer genitals to your inner reproductive organs.

Hair, There, Everywhere!

One of the for-real signs you're entering puberty is that you begin to grow hair in places that were once smooth as a baby's bottom. Some of it will sprout in your armpits. Some of it will grow in your pubic area, the place where your legs meet. The first hair you see probably will be light colored and soft in texture. Gradually it will become darker, thicker, and curlier. You might grow a lot of hair in this area, or you might not.

The color of your pubic hair will not necessarily match the hair on the rest of your body, particularly your head. As you grow older, though, it will turn gray just like the hair on your head. Pubic hair acts as a filter to keep dirt, particles, and other irritants out of the sensitive vulva area.

Don't worry that you'll wake up one morning to find a shag rug down there. Your pubic hair doesn't come in overnight. Like your breasts, it develops, for the average person, in five stages.

In **stage 1,** during pre-puberty, there is no pubic hair except for possibly a few fuzzy or downy hairs.

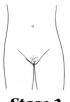

Stage 1

When puberty starts and you enter **stage 2,** the first real hairs begin to grow. These are straight and fine, and slightly dark in color.

Stage 2

Stage 3 sees the continued growth of hair, as it gets thicker, coarser, curlier, and possibly darker in color.

Stage 3

The hair becomes thicker and curlier and covers a larger area during **stage 4**.

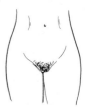

Stage 4

At the end of **stage 5,** the pubic hair is that of an adult's: thick, coarse, and tightly curled. It usually grows in the shape of an upside-down triangle. In some people, the hair continues to grow toward the belly button or down the insides of the thighs.

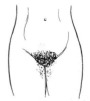

Stage 5

Most girls reach stage 3 between the ages of 11 and 13, and most start their periods at around this stage or stage 4. Keep in mind, though, that each girl is different. You'll develop at the pace that is right for you.

Behind the Scenes

While on the outside you are undergoing gradual changes during puberty, on the inside even more radical changes are taking place. Your reproductive organs, the body parts that enable you to become pregnant and grow a baby, are beginning to mature.

A woman's reproductive organs are the vagina, the fallopian tubes, the ovaries, and the uterus. Here is a description of each, along with a few body parts that do not belong to the reproductive system but are located in the same area.

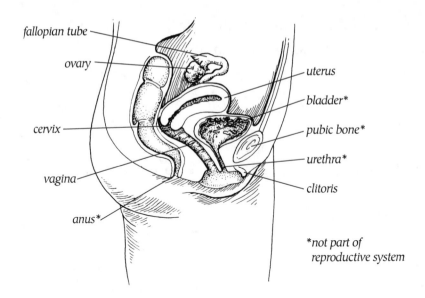

fallopian tube

ovary

cervix

vagina

anus*

uterus

bladder*

pubic bone*

urethra*

clitoris

*not part of
reproductive system

**Female Reproductive System
(cross section)**

The vagina

The vagina is a pouchlike structure that joins your body's external sex organs to your reproductive organs. The walls of the vagina are made of muscle and can stretch so that a tampon can be inserted and, during intercourse, a man's penis can fit inside. It channels your menstrual blood to the outside of your body. During childbirth, this passageway can expand large enough to allow a baby to pass through.

When you enter puberty, the walls of the vagina begin to secrete fluid, which you may see in the form of a milky or clear discharge on your underwear. After you have your first period, this discharge may become sticky or slippery, like egg whites, meaning you are probably going to ovulate soon.

Sexual arousal also causes this secretion, which lubricates the vaginal walls to make entry of the penis during intercourse easier. Your vagina may feel wet even if you're not sexually aroused. This is because once you reach puberty, the walls of your vagina shed cells at a faster rate, and the fluid is needed to flush these dead cells out of your body.

The ovaries

These two small, walnut-sized organs produce the *ovum,* or egg. When fertilized, the egg can develop into a fetus. At birth, a girl's ovaries already contain hundreds of thousands of *ova,* or eggs—all that she will ever have in her lifetime. Each one is about the size of a sharpened pencil tip. The eggs do not mature until puberty. The ovaries also produce estrogen, the hormone responsible for most of the physical changes you go through during puberty.

The uterus

It is inside this hollow organ, shaped like an upside-down pear and made of thick muscle, that a fetus develops. About the size of a fist, the uterus can expand dramatically to accommodate a growing baby. When not pregnant, a woman's uterus weighs about 2 ounces; at the end of a pregnancy it weighs 2 pounds—and that's not including the weight of a full-term baby.

The uterus has three layers. The innermost is the *endometrium,* a lining of tissue containing glands and blood vessels. This tissue builds up during menstruation in preparation to cushion and nourish a baby. At the end of each menstrual cycle, if there is no egg to fertilize, the lining is shed. The middle layer, called the *myometrium,* is muscle that contracts to expel blood and tissue during menstruation, and to help push out a baby at the end of a pregnancy. The smooth outer covering of the uterus is called the *serosa.*

The cervix

The cervix is the tiny opening that is the entrance from the vagina into the uterus.

The fallopian tubes

These tubelike structures are about the width of a strand of spaghetti and serve as a passageway for ova. The end of each tube is shaped like a funnel and is covered with tiny, hairlike projections called *fimbriae.* These projections act like fingers to grab the egg and pull it into the tubes so it can begin its journey to the uterus.

The anus

The anus is not a reproductive organ, but the opening through which feces, or solid waste, leave your body.

Making Sense of Menstruation

You've probably heard all kinds of slang words to describe it, but the proper term for having your period is *menstruation.* Getting your first period, known as *menarche,* means that your body theoretically has all the hormones it needs to get pregnant and have a baby. *Menarche* comes from the Latin word *menses,* meaning "month." Your *menstrual cycle* actually refers not just to the days that you're bleeding, but to the entire time leading up to and through those days. The days you actually bleed are referred to as your *period.*

Menarche can take place as young as age 8 or as old as age 16. Every girl's body has its own schedule. Whether you get your first period at 10, 11, or 14, you're normal.

> ### MENSTRUATION MYTHS
>
> The Greek physician Galen believed menstrual flow was leftover blood from food that women couldn't digest. Because of its odor, menstruating women also were once believed to make meat spoil and bread dough fall!

You've also probably heard that your period is supposed to come every month, but that's not true for everyone. First of all, after you start having your period, it may take a while for you to establish a regular cycle. Once you do, you'll most likely—but not always—menstruate every month. Some girls may always have irregular periods. It's not unusual at all.

You may have a period every 21 days or every 28, or even as far apart as every 45 days. You may have that first period and then skip several months before the next one. Just relax. Your body is going through a new experience, so it takes time for it to find its groove.

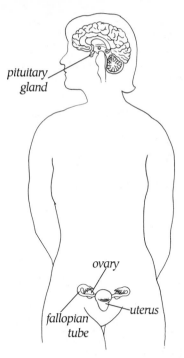

pituitary gland

ovary

fallopian tube

uterus

OK, So What's the Inside Scoop?

During puberty, your ovaries begin to increase in size. Next, your pituitary—the same gland that triggered puberty—puts out a hormone that travels through your bloodstream and into your ovaries. This hormone causes one of the eggs inside your ovary to ripen. Each egg is surrounded by a tiny fluid-filled sac called a *follicle*. The ripe ovum bursts out of the sac and is swept into the fallopian tube by the fimbriae. It then makes its way through the tube to the uterus. The process of the egg leaving the ovary is called *ovulation*.

In the meantime, the uterus is preparing a sort of "nest" for the ovum. The endometrium, the lining of the uterus, thickens with blood and cushioning tissue until ovulation occurs. If intercourse has taken place, sperm swim up through

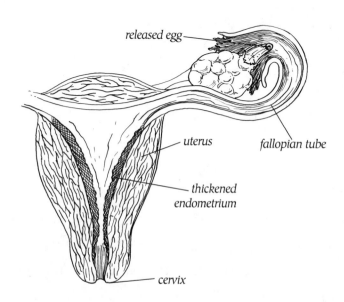

released egg

uterus

fallopian tube

thickened endometrium

cervix

TAKE TWO MENSES AND CALL ME IN THE MORNING

Menstrual blood is believed by many to have healing qualities. People in Morocco, in North Africa, have been known to apply menstrual blood to sores and wounds. The blood also has been used to treat gout (a disease similar to arthritis) and even menstrual disorders in the West!

the cervix and uterus and into the fallopian tubes, where one sperm may penetrate the egg and fertilize it. The egg then travels down and implants itself in the wall of the uterus, ready to develop into an embryo, then a fetus.

Most of the time, however, the egg is not fertilized. It then passes right through the uterus and disintegrates. Because a "nest" is not needed for the egg, the uterus sheds its built-up lining. This happens over a period of several days as the blood vessels inside the uterus weaken and slowly release their contents, which exit the body in the form of the menstrual flow that you see on your tampon or sanitary pad.

The amount of your own flow may look like a lot, but it really isn't as much as it seems. Some women's menstrual flow can be as little as a tablespoonful, while others flow as much as half a cup—which isn't all that much. Your flow may be heavy for just a day or two, then become lighter. Don't worry—you're not going to bleed to death. The blood may be thin and bright red, or thicker and brownish. You may see small clots of blood, particularly in the morning. Again, this is normal.

A period can last from two to seven days. You may have a period, however, that lasts three days one month and five days the next. Every girl and woman has a pattern that's right for her.

Although no one can predict the exact day you will have your first period, your tenth period, or whatever, there are some signs you can watch for. More than 60 percent of girls have their first period in stage 4 of pubic hair development. Others begin during stage 4 of breast development. Some girls may start having a clear discharge about six months before menarche. Others may begin menstruating at about the same time their mothers did. Ask your mom if she remembers how old she was.

BE PREPARED

That old Boy Scout motto is something to keep in mind when you think you're going to get your first period—or any period, if you've already gone through menarche. The commonsense rule is to carry a tampon or sanitary napkin in your backpack or purse. Most public restrooms have vending machines that dispense pads and tampons.

When you get your very first period, it won't be like somebody opened the floodgates. Most likely you'll see a bright red spot or a dark, sticky brownish stain on your underwear. So if you're caught without a tampon or pad when it happens, the blood won't soak through to your clothes. And despite what you may have heard, no one can tell just by looking at you that you're having your period.

Sanitary Pads

Pads and tampons are made of cotton and other absorbent material and are designed to catch and absorb your menstrual flow. They come in different sizes and thicknesses. Experiment to find the one that's right for you.

Sanitary pads have a strip of adhesive so you can stick them right on the inside of your underpants. They also have a plastic-like shield on the side that faces away from your body to help prevent blood from leaking out. On the days your flow is heavy, you may want to use a "maxi" pad, which is thicker than the "mini" pads usually used for lighter days.

It's a good idea to change your pad every three or four hours. Although menstrual blood is actually quite clean, a soaked pad can become uncomfortable and eventually will leak. Wrap the napkin in toilet tissue and put it in the wastepaper basket if you're at home. Public restrooms and those at your school have special receptacles for the disposal of pads. *Never* flush it down the toilet, even if the package says it's OK. It can clog the plumbing.

Tampons

A tampon is a rolled cylinder of absorbent material that is inserted into your vagina. It has a string attached to one end that hangs out of your vaginal opening after the tampon is inserted. To remove a used tampon, you just pull on the string. The tampon *cannot* magically work its way into your body and disappear into the uterus, because the muscles of your  vaginal wall hold it firmly in place. Besides, the opening of the cervix is way too small for a tampon to fit through and get into the uterus.

During the daytime, you should change your tampon every three to four hours whether your flow is light or heavy. Before going to bed at night, and whenever your flow is heavy, you may want to use a maxi or mini pad as a backup to catch any overflow. Like sanitary pads, wrap the tampon in toilet tissue and dispose of it properly instead of flushing it down the toilet.

It's a myth that a girl can't use a tampon if she's a virgin. The *hymen,* the thin membrane around the entrance to the vagina, has a small opening; if it didn't, menstrual blood wouldn't be able to flow through. Some women even have more than one opening. The hymen is made of stretchy material that can accommodate a tampon if it's inserted correctly.

However, some girls are not comfortable using a tampon and may prefer pads. The choice is up to you. If you think you're ready to try a tampon, it's best to wait until you have your period, because the blood flow will make it easier to glide the tampon in. Here are some tips:

❀ First, look at the drawing of the female reproductive organs on page 24. You'll see that your vagina slants up and toward your lower back. Be sure to insert the tampon in this direction.

❀ Start with a slender-size tampon that comes with an applicator. This will make the insertion process easier.

❀ Wash your hands thoroughly with soap and hot water. Remove the tampon's outer wrapping.

❀ You can insert the tampon standing, sitting, or lying down, whichever you find most comfortable for you. Using the first two fingers of one hand, pull back on the outer and inner lips covering the vagina. Hold the tampon in your other hand with your finger on the end that has the string attached. Put the tampon up to the vaginal opening.

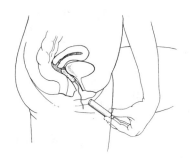

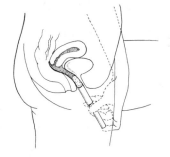

❀ Push the end of the tampon into your vagina, remembering to angle it up and back.

❀ Use your finger to push the inner applicator tube into the outer tube. This will push the tampon farther into your vagina and out of the applicator. Pull out the empty applicator, wrap it in tissue, and throw it away in a wastebasket.

Make certain you push the tampon in far enough. Once it's inside, you shouldn't feel it at all. An improperly inserted tampon will feel uncomfortable or even painful, particularly when you're sitting.

Don't be disappointed if you're not successful right away. Vaginal muscles are very tight at your age and can be resistant to insertion. Relax, try again, and if it still doesn't work, just stick on a pad and wait until next time. You might want to ask your mom or an older friend to help you out.

Write It Down!

If you want to be as prepared as possible for your period, try keeping a calendar. Record the first day of bleeding on the calendar, and do this for the next several months until you see a pattern start to emerge. Remember, though, that your period may not become regular right away, and in some cases may never become regular.

Toxic Shock Syndrome

Toxic shock syndrome (TSS) is a serious but rare infection. Most people who have contracted TSS are women who were menstruating and using tampons.

TSS is caused by a bacterium called *Staphylococcus aureus* that lives on your skin and in your body's warm, moist cavities. Normally, this bacterium is harmless, but it grows and multiplies in a blood-soaked environment, namely a tampon, until it produces a toxin. Symptoms of TSS include diarrhea, sore throat and achy muscles, and a fever of 101 degrees or higher. If you develop any of these symptoms while using tampons, see your doctor as soon as possible.

It's believed that leaving a tampon in for long periods of time has caused TSS in some women. Be smart: Wash your hands thoroughly before inserting a tampon, and change it regularly—every three or four hours.

Quit Yer Bellyachin'

Lots of theories exist as to why girls and women have menstrual cramps—that pain and heaviness you feel in your lower abdomen before or during your period—but no one knows for sure what causes them. Some girls may have more severe cramps, others more mild. Some girls may never experience cramps at all. To help make cramps more bearable, practice the following:

* Get enough rest—at least seven or eight hours of sleep each night.

* Drink plenty of water. It doesn't have to be eight glasses a day exactly. Just get in the habit, and carry a bottle of water around with you so you don't forget.

* Eat well. That means lots of green, leafy vegetables. Lay off the salty foods! They'll make your body retain water and feel even more uncomfortable.

If you do get mild cramps, try going for a brisk walk or some other form of exercise that's not too strenuous. Or, lie down and place a heating pad or hot-water bottle on your abdomen. For more severe cramps, check with your doctor and ask whether you can take an aspirin or ibuprofen tablet. If your cramps are extremely painful—so much that you need to stay home from school—make an appointment with your doctor right away.

HONORABLE DISCHARGE

Discharges—fluids released from your vagina—are common among girls approaching puberty and even among adult women. It's one of the ways your body cleanses itself. Your cervix contains glands that release mucus that flows through and out the vagina. On the way, the mucus picks up dead cells from the vagina, much like the dead cells that your skin is constantly shedding.

The discharge may be clear, milky, or white, and stringy or slippery to the touch. This is perfectly normal. However, if you notice a strong, unpleasant odor, if the discharge is greenish, yellowish, or grayish in color, or if it causes itching or redness on your vulva, see a doctor. You may have a vaginal infection. This type of infection is not serious if caught early, but it needs to be treated as soon as possible.

Vaginal itching has a variety of other causes. Some common ones:

- ✿ Wearing underwear that is not 100 percent cotton or does not have a cotton crotch.

- ✿ Wearing a wet swimsuit for a long period of time. Don't sit around in your swimsuit after you get out of the pool.

- ✿ Wearing jeans, pants, tights, exercise wear, or leggings that are too tight. If you have to squeeze yourself into those Gap jeans, buy the next size up.

- ✿ Being allergic to soaps, detergents, and bubble bath.

THE MOODY BLUES

Some girls—but not all—feel different than usual from one week to about ten days before they start their periods. They experience mood changes—everything from being filled with energy to feeling depressed and blue, as though nothing seems to be going right. They may feel so tense they're about to burst, or so confident they can do anything.

weepy   grumpy   puffy

The changes can be physical as well. Some girls feel bloated, and others may have swelling in their hands, wrists, ankles, or feet. Backaches or cramps are common, along with tender or sore breasts and nipples. Chalk it all up to premenstrual syndrome (PMS).

Doctors aren't sure what exactly causes PMS. Some believe it's brought on by a vitamin or nutritional deficiency, others think it's because the body isn't creating as many hormones as usual. Whatever the cause, you've got it and you just want to know what you can do about it. Here are some tips that may help you feel better.

✿ Eat less sugary foods.

✿ Eat balanced meals that include more green, leafy vegetables; whole grains; and nuts and seeds.

✿ If you're a caffeine nut, cut way, way back on your intake of colas (yes, they contain caffeine—lots of it), tea, and coffee. Better yet, eliminate caffeine completely. No more lattes or mochas! Think juice, water, or herbal tea.

✿ Move that body! Get out and work out. Jog, shoot some hoops, go in-line skating, clean up the yard, take the dog for a walk. Don't go overboard; just do an activity you enjoy.

If you have mild PMS symptoms, the above tips should help. If your symptoms are more severe and make you feel really miserable, consult your doctor.

CHAPTER 3

Boys II Men

The last time I had to give a speech in class, I got a
hard-on. It happened right in the middle of my talk,
and I wasn't even thinking about sex! I didn't know
what to do. I was so embarrassed. I thought everyone
could see it.

—Antonio, age 13

Ask your buddies what puberty is like, and they'll probably shrug and say it's no
big deal, probably even crack a lame joke. But if you talked to one of those same
guys alone, he'd probably sing a different tune. He may be a lot more curious
about what's happening to his body than he'd care to admit in front of his pals.

You've Got Male

When the pituitary gland signals your body that it's time for puberty to begin, you
go through a series of physical—and emotional—changes, just like girls do. You're
on your way to maturing into an adult, both physically and sexually. You're not a
boy anymore; you're entering the preteen and teen years. Your body shape will
change, and your sexual organs will begin to develop. Even though you probably

aren't planning on having children in the near future, your sperm production will increase, making it possible for you to father a child.

The onset of puberty in boys usually is between the ages of 12 and 14, but it can take place earlier or later. Whatever time it happens to you is normal for *you*. The illustration at right shows the average boy's body at two different ages.

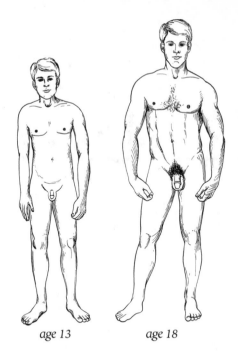

age 13   *age 18*

In the following list, you might find questions you've been wanting to ask. They're answered in the text that follows.

✿ My best friend is my age, and he's starting to look like a grown-up already. How much longer am I going to look like a kid?

✿ Almost all the girls in my class are taller than me. Talk about inferiority complexes! Will I ever catch up?

✿ I'm going to my doctor for an annual checkup. I'd like to ask him a couple of questions about my penis. What's the right name for everything?

✿ A guy on my basketball team has a penis that looks different from mine. I always thought all guys were the same down there. What's going on?

✿ One of my testicles hangs lower than the other. Is this OK?

✿ I have bumps on my scrotum. Is something wrong with me?

✿ When will I start growing a beard? I'm 15 and all my friends already shave.

✿ What's an erection, and how does it happen?

✿ The other night I woke up and thought I'd wet the bed. My dad said I had a "wet dream," but he didn't explain what it meant. What is it? Is it normal?

✿ I keep getting this itchy rash between my legs. What is it?

✿ I'm 13 and my voice is starting to change. It's really embarrassing. Whenever I answer the phone, people think I'm my sister. When will my voice stop "cracking"?

The Big Picture

If you look at your body and then look at an adult male's body, you'll see a big difference. The grown-up's body is taller, has bigger muscles, and has broader shoulders that make the hips seem narrow in comparison. Your body will undergo these same changes as you move through puberty on your way to becoming a man.

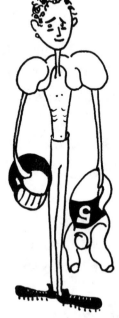

During this time, you'll experience your biggest growth spurt. In other words, you'll grow faster than you ever will again. You may even grow as much as 4 or 5 inches in a year! While you're gaining in height, other radical changes are happening inside and outside your body.

Your muscles will increase in size, and your sex organs will grow larger, too. You'll find hair growing where you didn't have any, or had very little, before. Some guys seem to speed right through puberty, while others develop more slowly. If the height of some of the girls in your class has you a little worried, don't be. It's not known why, but many girls begin their growth spurt a couple of years earlier than most guys. Relax. You'll catch up in no time.

Talk the Talk

One of the first signs that you're entering puberty is that your *genitals*—your penis and testicles—are getting larger. Another sign is that you begin to grow pubic hair around your genitals. A lot of guys have particular names for their genitals that you wouldn't use if you were talking to your own mother. These names may be hip, and it's OK to use them if they make you feel more comfortable, but it's also cool to know the correct medical terms. You'll be glad you know them when you're talking with your doctor—or your parents. Read on and study the accompanying illustrations.

Below are terms that describe your outer sexual organs and their parts.

The penis

The penis is the male sex organ through which both semen and urine pass. One half of your penis actually is hidden inside your body. This half reaches almost to the anus and is attached just under your pelvis.

The shaft

The long part of the penis that connects the glans to your body is called the shaft.

The glans

The glans is the tip, or head, of the penis. *Glans* is the Latin word for "acorn," which describes its shape.

The corona

The ridge of bumpy skin surrounding the glans is referred to as the corona.

The foreskin

This is the fold of skin that covers the glans. Now, some of you know exactly what we're talking about, and some of you may be thinking about what you look like down there and saying, "What fold of skin?" If you're in the latter group, you're probably *circumcised.*

All boys are born with a foreskin. Often, it is surgically removed a day or two after birth by a doctor during a procedure called *circumcision.* Boys whose families belong to the Jewish or Muslim faith undergo this procedure because it is required by these religions. In the United States, most boys are circumcised for a number of reasons. Some parents have it done for hygienic reasons, because they claim it is easier to keep a circumcised penis clean than an uncircumcised penis. Others have it done simply because it has become a common practice. More and more parents, however, are electing not to have their sons circumcised.

Whether you have the circumcised or uncircumcised model, both work the same way. And if you're a girl reading this section and curious, the foreskin just looks like a flap that covers the tip of the penis. That's it. The guy simply moves or lifts it when he urinates. When the penis becomes erect, the foreskin is naturally pushed aside to allow for the ejaculation, or discharge, of sperm.

The scrotum

The scrotum is the loose sac of skin and involuntary muscles (those you can't consciously control) located under the penis. Inside the scrotum are your testicles. As a baby, the skin of the scrotum is smooth; as you reach maturity, it becomes thicker and wrinkled. The scrotum protects the testicles. If you jump into cold water, for instance, your scrotum pulls your testicles up toward your body, where it is warmer. In hot weather, or if you become overheated, the scrotum relaxes, moving your testicles farther away from the body.

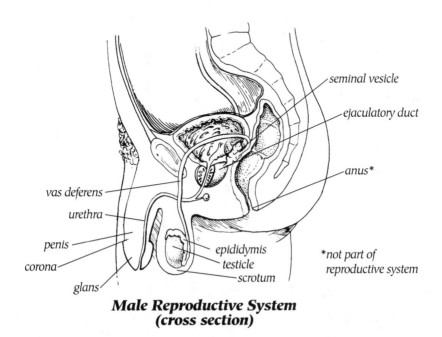

Male Reproductive System
(cross section)

The following terms describe your internal reproductive organs.

The testicles

The two egg-shaped organs inside the scrotum are called *testicles,* or *testes.* Inside each testicle are more than 200 compartments. Inside each compartment are threadlike tubes called *seminiferous tubules,* where sperm—the male sex cells that fertilize a woman's ovum, or egg—are produced.

Testicles also make *testosterone,* the hormone that tells your body to begin developing adult male characteristics such as facial and body hair. Testosterone also triggers the growth of your penis, scrotum, and the testicles themselves.

One testicle may grow faster than the other, which is perfectly normal. One also hangs lower than the other; this prevents the testicles from crashing into each other when you're walking or running. But don't think this is reason enough for not wearing a cup or jockstrap when you're in gym class or playing sports. If you've ever been hit in the testicles, you know it's not pretty.

The sperm

Not really an organ, these are tiny, microscopic sex cells produced in the testicles. Each sperm has a head and a long, whiplike tail. Each day

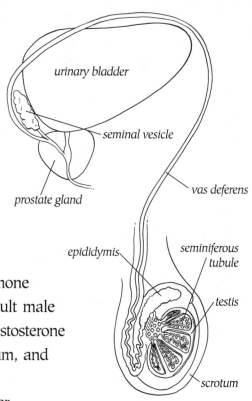

Cross Section of a Testicle

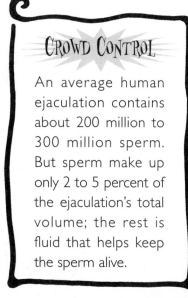

CROWD CONTROL

An average human ejaculation contains about 200 million to 300 million sperm. But sperm make up only 2 to 5 percent of the ejaculation's total volume; the rest is fluid that helps keep the sperm alive.

the testicles produce millions of new sperm and will continue to do so until you reach old age. Fertilization takes place when a sperm penetrates a woman's ovum.

The epididymis

The long, coiled tube attached to the back of the each testicle is the epididymis. If uncoiled, the tube would stretch about 20 feet. Sperm travel from the testicle through the epididymis over the course of several weeks until they mature, then are stored in the ampulla. If you gently feel the back of your testicle through your scrotum, you'll find a soft, raised ridge—this is the epididymis.

The vas deferens

This is the tube that transports sperm from the epididymis to the urethra. Each testicle has its own vas deferens.

The ampulla

The enlarged end of the vas deferens is the ampulla. Also called *Henle's ampulla*, it is where mature sperm are stored until they leave the body.

The seminal vesicles

A pair of glands shaped like dragonfly wings, the seminal vesicles are connected to each vas deferens. The vesicles produce most of the milky white fluid that makes up semen, which is discharged, along with the sperm, during ejaculation.

The prostate

The prostate is a doughnut-shaped gland surrounding the urethra and located under the bladder. The prostate also adds fluid to semen.

The urethra

This is the tube through which urine from the bladder and semen from the repro-ductive organs exits the penis. The urethra in a male is approximately 9 inches long. Only one fluid can pass through the urethra at a time. If semen is being released, a tiny valve shuts off the urine flow, and during urination, a tiny valve stops the flow of semen.

A Hairy Issue

Testosterone, the hormone that causes your genitals to become larger, also tells your body to start growing hair on parts of your body other than your head.

First, you'll probably notice hair growing in the area between your legs, called the pubic region. These hairs will be soft and downy at first and will gradually become coarser, thicker, and curlier. If you notice bumps on your scrotum, don't be alarmed—in a short while little strands of hair will sprout from them.

The development of the penis and growth of pubic hair occurs over five stages.

Stage 1 is the pre-puberty stage from birth through childhood. You have no pubic hair except maybe a few strands. If you notice some hair, it will look and feel the same as the hair on your belly or legs—soft and smooth. No dark and curlies yet. Your penis, scrotum, and testicles will not change much.

Stage 1

You enter *stage 2* when puberty begins. The main change is in your testicles. They have been growing ever since pre-puberty, but at a very, very slow rate. Now they start to grow a little faster, causing the scrotum to hang lower and become looser and more wrinkly. The skin in your genital area may get a little darker or redder. You won't notice much change in the size of your penis. Some guys start growing pubic hair at this stage, some don't.

Stage 2

Stage 3: OK, now it's the penis's turn. As you can see in the illustration, it's longer and wider than the previous two stages. The scrotum and testicles continue to grow. Often the larger testicle

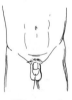

Stage 3

hangs lower. The skin of the penis and scrotum becomes darker. If your pubic hair hasn't come in yet, it probably will start now. The first hairs sprout around the base of the penis, where it attaches to your body. They may be hard to see and may not be dark or curly, but eventually they will be. Hair also will grow on your scrotum and around the anus.

Don't freak if you find bumps on your penis or scrotum that do not sprout hairs. Those are oil and sweat glands that have been turned on by puberty. That's why you may feel moist and smell a little different down there.

Your penis, scrotum, and testicles continue to develop through **stage 4.** You'll probably have quite a bit of pubic hair by this time, and it will continue to get curlier, coarser, and darker. It usually grows in an upside-down triangle pattern and spreads upward toward your belly button and down toward your thighs.

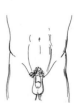

Stage 4

Stage 5 is the fully grown stage; however, your pubic hair may continue to grow until you're about 20.

Stage 5

Many boys are 16 when they reach stage 5, but as with any average, some boys will reach it when they are younger and some when they are older. You won't look *exactly* like any of the stages illustrated here. More likely you will be in between. They've been provided here as a general guideline of what you can expect.

Not every boy hits every stage at the same speed or time. You may zip from stage 3 to stage 5 and skip stage 4 altogether, or you may move more slowly through each.

Short Story

The hairs that grow in your pubic area are called *terminal hairs.* They grow only an inch or two maximum, then they fall out and new ones start to grow.

Genes Whiz!

How much body hair you eventually grow—on your chest, arms, legs, back, and under your arms—depends on your *genes*. Technically, a gene is a unit of hereditary material found inside a cell. Genes determine particular features, for example, your hair color or body type. Each  human cell holds more than 50,000 different genes. Half of all your genes are inherited from your mother, and half come from your father, through the egg and sperm.

Guys who come from families that have lots of body hair will most likely be pretty hairy themselves. If the male members of your family have only a small amount of hair on their chests, arms, and legs, you'll probably have a similar amount yourself. Sometime after you begin growing pubic hair, you'll notice that you are developing hair in your armpits, and that the hair on your arms and legs is getting thicker.

Curious about when that peach fuzz is going to appear on your face? Facial hair usually doesn't appear until the later stages of puberty, or somewhere around ages 14 to 16. Some guys don't sprout whiskers until they're 19 or 20, so don't sweat it if you can't get that goatee going yet. Like your pubic hair, the hair on your face may be the same color as the hair on your head, or it may be lighter or darker.

Boys and...Boobs?

You probably already know that puberty is the time when a girl's breasts begin to develop. What you may not realize is that guys also have breasts, and that these go through changes as well. It's all totally normal. Your nipples will enlarge, and the areola—the ring of skin around the nipple—will get darker and wider.

Doctors say it's not unusual for a guy's breasts to swell somewhat during puberty. In fact, more than 50 percent of guys experience this. Your breasts may even feel sore or tender at times, which is also normal. It won't last, so don't think you'll need to go bra shopping anytime soon.

You may notice a lump under your nipple. This is a fairly common occurrence, and happens to 40 to 60 percent of boys. Although it is possible for boys and men to get breast cancer, most lumps are not cancerous in guys going through puberty, and they disappear after a couple of years. Just to be on the safe side, though, have your doctor examine any lumps or irregularities.

All About Erections

"Having an erection" is the phrase used to describe your penis when it becomes hard, stiff, and straight.

Here's how an erection happens. Your penis contains nerves, spongy tissue (corpus cavernosum and corpus spongiosum), muscles, erection chambers (which look like two long balloons), and blood vessels. When a guy becomes sexually aroused, arteries—the vessels that pump blood away from your heart and to the rest of the body—send blood rushing into the penis. An erect penis contains four to six times the amount of blood in a nonerect penis. The spongy tissue and the erection chambers fill with blood because the veins—the vessels that return blood to the heart—located at the base of the penis are squeezed shut by tiny muscles.

The blood trapped in the penis causes it to harden and rise. When erect, the penis points up and away from your body, almost straight up in some cases or at various angles in between. Any position is normal.

Erections are sometimes referred to as "boners." Even though the penis gets hard, it contains no bones. The erection is caused by the blood rushing into the penis.

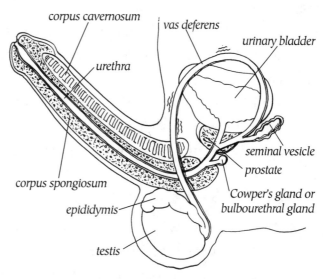

Cross Section of Erectile Tissue

At some point, the muscles around the veins relax, causing the excess blood to flow out through the open veins and back into the body. The penis then returns to its soft, relaxed form.

Many things can cause an erection, and not all of them have to do with thinking sexy thoughts. Ultrasound pictures inside a mother's womb have shown that even unborn baby boys can have erections.

Sometimes a penis becomes erect when a guy isn't even thinking about sex, or anything arousing for that matter. A *spontaneous erection* can happen all on its own and can last for a couple of minutes or longer. Some guys report having this type of erection only once in a while; others say they have them frequently, as often as a dozen times a day. It's no doubt embarrassing if you're at school or in a public place, but take heart, people don't seem to notice—really. Keep in mind it's a normal part of puberty.

WET DREAMS MAY COME

Imagine this: You wake up in the middle of the night and feel a wet spot on your pajamas or bedsheet. Your first thought is that you've wet the bed. Embarrassment ensues. Good thing the lights aren't on.

What really happened is that you, like most guys, had a "wet dream." The technical term is *nocturnal emission, nocturnal* meaning "during the night" and *emission* meaning "to send out." Semen was ejaculated, or discharged, from your penis during the night. Just as you have no control over a spontaneous erection, you can't keep a wet dream from happening. They are perfectly normal and common, and not a cause for worry. Just get out of bed, change clothes, and go back to sleep.

Testicular Self-Exam

From watching reports on television, you know doctors recommend that girls and women examine their breasts once a month as a way of preventing breast cancer. What isn't reported as often in the media is that testicular self-examination for guys is *equally* important.

Performing this simple examination each month is a proven way of detecting testicular cancer early. Left untreated, testicular cancer can spread to other parts of the body. If it's found at an early stage, it can be stopped in its tracks. It's unlikely that a guy your age will get testicular cancer, but it's wise to get into the habit of checking *now*.

First, place your hand on the back of your scrotum and feel for the epididymis, the soft, tubelike structure behind the testicle. This is so you won't mistake it for a suspicious lump. Then, follow these steps:

✿ Take a hot shower or bath, which will soften the skin of the scrotum. Then stand in front of a mirror. Look at your scrotum in the mirror and check for any swelling in the skin.

✿ Examine each testicle using both hands. Place your index and middle fingers under the testicle with your thumbs on top.

✿ Your testicle should feel rubbery and smooth, like a peeled hard-boiled egg. Gently roll each testicle between your fingers and thumbs, checking for lumps, hardness, or any irregularities. You should not feel any pain during this procedure. Don't be alarmed if one testicle feels slightly larger than the other; this is normal. If you notice a sudden change in size, however, tell a parent and notify your doctor.

✿ If you find a lump or irregularity, make an appointment with your doctor. Although many irregularities are not likely to be cancerous, it's best to let an expert make that call.

See a doctor if you notice any of these other warning signs:

✿ Pain in a testicle.

✿ Abnormal enlargement of a testicle.

❁ Reduction in size of a testicle.

❁ A feeling of heaviness in your scrotum.

❁ A dull ache in your lower abdomen or groin area (the area around your genitals).

❁ A sudden collection of fluid in your scrotum.

❁ Blood in your urine, or pain while you're urinating.

The Itchy and Scratchy Show

You don't have to be an athlete to get the condition known as *jock itch*. Jock itch is an infection of the skin in the genital area. The medical term for jock itch is *tinea cruris*. It is caused by certain kinds of fungi, microscopic organisms that grow in warm, moist environments. If you have a preference for wearing tight pants, for example, you are creating the ideal living conditions for the fungi that cause jock itch.

To avoid getting this uncomfortable, itchy rash, practice the following:

❁ Wear clean briefs or boxer shorts with a comfortable fit to allow air to circulate around your genitals.

❁ Don't wear tight-fitting jeans or pants.

❁ Dry yourself thoroughly, particularly in the genital area, after showering or swimming.

❁ Don't sit around in a wet Speedo or other tight-fitting swimsuit. They may be sexy, but jock itch is not.

❁ Don't wear a sweaty or dirty jockstrap. Make sure yours is washed frequently.

Handle with Care

It's now the law almost everywhere that anyone who rides a motorcycle or bicycle must wear a helmet. If you play a contact sport, ride a skateboard, or in-line skate, you already know that you need protective gear—a helmet or elbow and knee pads, for example—to keep your brain inside your head and your other body parts intact.

Your penis and testicles deserve the same sort of protection. Cycling is a sport that puts your genitals at particular risk. What would happen if you had to stop suddenly and slid off the seat of your bike and landed on the bar? Not only would you suffer a painful injury, but you also could do permanent

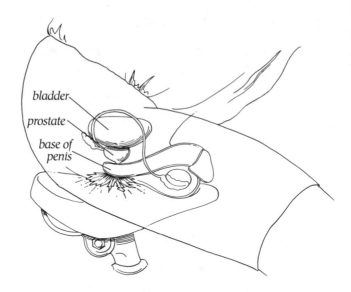

Bicycle Injury to Penis and Prostate

damage to your penis and testicles. A crushing blow to either of these parts, or to the *perineum*—the area between the base of the penis and your anus—may result in impotence, which means never being able to have an erection again, or to have sexual intercourse, or to father children.

If you haven't already done so, march immediately to your nearest bike shop or sporting-goods store and buy padding for the bar of your bicycle. Professional cyclists don't race without a padded bar, and you shouldn't ride without one either.

Here are more tips from doctors who treat penile injuries: *Don't* ride your bike down steps. If you must ride on a rough road, stand up in the bike's stirrups, or even better, *walk* your bike over these areas.

If your bicycle seat isn't comfortable, you might want to replace it with the new wedge-shaped seat to keep the pressure off your privates. You'll also find this at bike shops and sporting-goods stores.

The next time you're off to play hockey, tennis, baseball, or any other sport, take that cup or jockstrap out of your drawer and put it on. You won't be a wimp—professional athletes protect themselves and you should, too.

The Sound and the Worry

Sometime during puberty—no one knows exactly when—your voice will begin to change. Without your even trying, your voice will start to sound deeper, as if it belongs to a grown-up. Your voice may deepen over a period of time—so gradually that you don't even notice it's changing—and never revert back to your "boy" voice. Or, like some guys, you may go back and forth, sounding "manly" one minute and squeaky and high-pitched the next.

This "cracking" may make you feel self-conscious at first, but it won't last. And it probably won't happen nearly as often as you're afraid it might. For instance, it may pop up only when you're trying to reach a high note when you're singing. And a lot of guys don't experience *any* cracking. So unless you belong to a choir or vocal group, don't worry about it. And if you do, it's still no reason to clam up. Hey, look at it this way: it probably happened to every single one of the Backstreet Boys.

You can thank the hormone testosterone for causing your voice to become lower and deeper. It's what signals your *larynx*—your voice box—to grow larger and your vocal cords to lengthen and thicken, which is what makes the pitch of your voice lower.

The larynx is located in your throat between your *pharynx* (the upper part of your airway) and your *trachea* (your windpipe, which leads to the lungs). It creates your voice through the *vocal cords,* which run down the center. At the top is a flap called the *epiglottis,* which prevents food from getting into your airway. Your Adam's apple, which is more prominent in boys than in girls, is made of cartilage.

Look—or rather, listen—for this change between ages 14 and 16. But again, it could happen sooner or later than that.

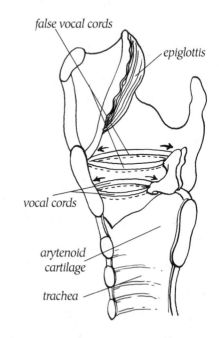

false vocal cords

epiglottis

vocal cords

arytenoid cartilage

trachea

Cross Section of Throat

CHAPTER 4

The Good, the Bad, and the B.O.

I'm the only one in my group of friends to not have much body hair. All the other girls' underarms and legs—even their pubic hair, some of them say—are getting bushier. They say I'm lucky I don't have to think about shaving, but I still feel left out. I think I'm going to look like a kid forever.

—Tina, age 15

If you've read the chapters on girls' and guys' bodies, you already know how different you are from the opposite sex—and we mean that in a good way. But in some ways, though, you're all in the same boat. Bad skin, bad hair, and bad B.O. don't discriminate; one or all of them happen to just about everyone. (Of course, you may know someone who has clear skin and perfect hair and always smells minty fresh, but they're probably some sort of alien anyway, so they don't count.)

Whatever crisis you're going through—and despite what adults may say, it is a crisis to you—it helps to know that you're not the only one experiencing it, and that this, too, shall pass.

Again, here's a list of frequently asked questions about changes in your body that all teens go through. You've probably had one or more of them in mind for a while, and have been reluctant or embarrassed to ask them. Yeah, yeah, we all know the drill by now: "No question is a dumb question," and "How are you going to learn if you don't ask?" But let's face it—sometimes you're just uncomfortable asking. So we've answered them in the text that follows.

✿ I thought you only get pimples on your face, but I've got them on my back, too! Is this normal?

✿ Both my mom and dad told me they had acne when they were teenagers. My dad said he had it pretty bad. Will that happen to me, too?

✿ When I was 13 I had perfect hair. I hardly ever needed to wash it. Now I'm almost 15 and my hair is oily and limp all the time. What can I do?

✿ Why do I sweat so much? Even when it's cold out, I get drippy under my arms. It soaks through my clothes and embarrasses me. My hands sweat, too, and I'm not even nervous.

✿ What's the difference between deodorant for men and deodorant for women?

✿ My aunt has big, brown freckles on her back and shoulders. She calls them sunspots. Will I get them, too?

✿ I've been told I should wear sunblock or sunscreen, but I've heard putting stuff like that on my skin can clog my pores and cause acne. Is this true?

Facing the Facts

Zits happen. There, we've said it. Now, how you deal with it is up to you.

If you've already had your first breakout, you've no doubt asked yourself, Why me? Well, you're not alone. According to dermatologists—medical doctors who treat skin conditions—85 of every 100 people between the ages of 12 and 25 get acne.

The good news is that although almost everyone gets acne, it can be controlled. We don't know what causes acne, but we do know that it's a disorder of the skin's hair follicles and oil-producing glands, called the *sebaceous glands*. During childhood these glands were small and produced only small amounts of an oily substance called *sebum*. This oil flows through your hollow hair follicles and out through your pores—very tiny openings—where it softens and lubricates your skin.

Then puberty struck. Your hormones cracked the whip on your sebaceous glands ("Hey! Get moving. These teens don't have enough turmoil in their lives!")

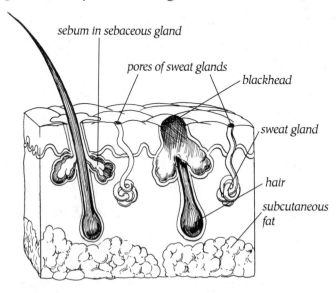

sebum in sebaceous gland

pores of sweat glands

blackhead

sweat gland

hair

subcutaneous fat

Cross Section of Skin with Blackhead

and caused them to grow larger and produce more oil. The oil that cannot escape through your pores becomes trapped in the follicle and forms a plug. The clogged pore turns into a whitehead, a blackhead, or a pimple. A whitehead is a plug that doesn't break through to the skin's surface. A blackhead is a plug that pokes through to the surface and becomes dark when the sebum is exposed to air. It is not created by a piece of dirt that got into the plug, as that know-it-all kid in class may have told you. If bacteria are present on your skin, they feed on the clogged sebum, causing an infection that results in a pimple.

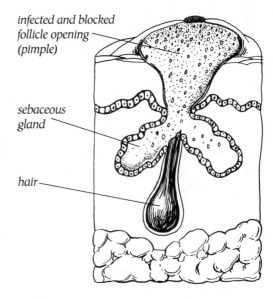

If your pores clog easily, you're a candidate for developing pimples. You have sebaceous glands all over your body, but the areas that are most zit-prone are your face, neck, shoulders, upper arms, and back.

Cross Section of Skin with Pimple

WOULD YOU LIKE FRIES WITH YOUR ZITS?

Contrary to what you may have heard, eating chocolate, french fries, or other greasy or salty foods is *not* the major cause of pimples. If you find that a certain food seems to make you break out, however, eliminate it from your diet and see what happens.

Stress—positive or negative—can play a role in outbreaks. Now you know why you seem to get a huge zit just before that important exam or that big dance where you're hoping to catch the eye of a special someone. Also, hormonal changes, like the ones that occur just before a girl gets her period, can trigger an increase in blemishes.

Most of the time, though, you can chalk up your skin condition—smooth or pimply—to heredity. Simply put, if one or both of your parents or your older brother or sister had acne, you probably will, too. You may experience only a few pimples every once in a while, but most teens find that they break out in waves that come and go. And severe cases of acne may put you at risk of scarring. If yours is severe, consult your doctor or dermatologist. There are prescription medications that can provide relief.

PIMPLE PATROL

There's no surefire way to actually prevent pimples, but there are some things you can do that can help. Whether you have outbreaks often or just occasionally, you should take care of your skin in the following ways.

Keep it clean. Two or three times a day, gently wash your pimple-prone areas with mild soap and warm water, using your fingertips or a soft washcloth. Ivory soap or any antibacterial soap will work. Be sure to rinse off all the soap residue and pat your skin dry with a clean towel. As a substitute for soap and water you can use astringent, which is a non-oily facial cleanser applied with a cotton ball or square. If you have an oily back, wash with a soft back brush.

Blot that oil. For extra-oily skin, use a tissue to blot oil off your face several times a day.

Keep your hair off your face. Your hair can irritate acne by transferring dirt and oil to your skin. Wash your hair frequently and try to keep it off your face as much as possible, especially at night. If you have long hair, tie it back or put it up before going to bed.

Loosen up. The friction from sweatbands, baseball caps, tight-fitting helmets, and backpacks can cause irritation and make acne worse.

Don't sweat it. Perspiration is an irritant as well. After engaging in an activity that makes you sweat, bathe or shower with antibacterial soap.

Don't pop those pimples. We know it's oh so tempting—especially when that zit is ripe for the picking—but squeezing a pimple or touching a pimple-prone area transfers bacteria on your fingers to the area, causing more irritation and possibly scarring. Picking or popping a zit can leave a permanent red or brown spot even after the pimple has healed. There. Consider yourself warned.

Don't scrub. Scrubbing your pimples spreads infection and is almost as destructive as popping them. Gently wash instead.

Avoid certain products. Skin-care products that contain oil of any kind, such as cocoa butter, worsen acne. The same goes for hair sprays and hair gels. Read the labels of all products before you put them on your skin or hair. Look for a product that is oil-free or *noncomedogenic*—which means it will not clog pores—or designed for acne-prone skin.

Grease Is the Word

If it's not one thing, it's another. Just when you're bummed out by that first zit popping up on your facial plane, you notice your hair is, well, not itself these days. Where it was once normal and easy to take care of, it's now oily and has zero body.

Blame it on those sebaceous glands, the same ones that cause your face to break out. They're practically working overtime, coughing out oil on your head as well as on your face, back, and shoulders.

To get the greasies under control, wash your hair often—every day if you have to. If you have bangs, you might want to wash them more often to keep them looking good. Bangs not only pick up oil from your scalp, but they also get an extra dose from the oil on your forehead. So if you want to grow bangs to cover the zits on your forehead, think again. Each picks up oil from the other.

Your regular shampoo or any mild shampoo should do. Using a product that's designated for oily hair may help, but despite what the labels say, sometimes there's not much difference among shampoos for oily, normal, and dry hair. Avoid products that contain alcohol as an ingredient, which can dry out your hair.

Switch shampoos often, especially if you have a dandruff problem. Your hair can become too accustomed to the same brand, making it less effective. This doesn't mean you have to buy a new shampoo every week, though. Keep two brands on hand and alternate.

RAISING YOUR HACKLES

You may be surprised to know that your hair—at least the part of it that you can see—is dead. Dead cells, to be exact. The alive part is actually under your scalp, in the follicles. The follicles produce two types of hair. *Vellus* hair is the soft hair that covers most of your body. *Terminal* hair is the thicker, colored hair that grows on your scalp, eyebrows, and eyelashes, and in your armpits and pubic area during puberty.

Every hair on your body has a genetic code that determines its length. For example, the follicles on your scalp are genetically engineered to grow hair up to 40 inches long, whereas the hair in your pubic area grows only an inch or two at most. So if you were to transplant a scalp follicle into your pubic area, you would grow a long scalp hair there. (As if you'd want to.)

The color of your hair depends on the amount of *melanin,* a pigment, in the hair shaft. The texture of your hair is determined by the shape of the follicle. Round follicles produce straight hair; oval follicles grow curly hair; and kidney-shaped follicles sprout wavy hair.

ROOM TO GROW

There are about 300,000 hairs on your scalp at any given time. The exact number depends on how many hair follicles you are born with. Each day, male or female, you shed 100 to 150 hairs from your head. These are replaced by new hairs.

The experts aren't sure exactly why we grow hair, and why such a big mop of it sprouts on our heads. Some believe it was simply to keep dust and dirt out of our eyes. Others say it was to attract a mate. And to go the evolutionary route, some believe prehistoric humans grew a lot of body hair to protect themselves from the harsh elements, but once we became civilized and realized, "Hey, why not kill small animals and use *their* hair to cover ourselves?" our hairy coats were about as useful as the Cro-Magnon version of a leisure suit.

TOSS YOUR HAIR, DARLING

So how do you get your hair to look just like you see on the models in those magazine ads? Get real. Unless you're constantly under perfect lighting, with a hair-and-makeup artist attached at the hip, your hair will *not* look like you see in the ads. But if you want a plain old healthy, shiny head of hair, the following practices can help.

Don't overdo it. Too much heat, sun, or chlorine, or using hairstyling products to excess can dry out and damage the hair shafts. Brittle, frizzy, dull hair is the result. Wear a cap or hat if you're going to be in the sun or heat for long periods of time. If you swim in a pool, rinse your hair out thoroughly right after you get out, and shampoo it as soon as you can. Chlorine, over time, can tint your hair green.

Keep it clean. Unless you have a really dry scalp, it's wise to wash your hair every day or every other day with a mild shampoo. If your scalp is very dry, rinse it with warm water one day and shampoo it the next. Before you wash, brush your hair gently to loosen dirt, oil, and product residue and to stimulate your scalp.

Use a conditioner. This goes for guys as well as girls. It's not a "girly" thing; conditioner adds moisturizer, protein, and sometimes sunscreen to your hair. It needs to stay on for just a couple of minutes, so shampoo first, rinse, then apply conditioner and let it work while you're soaping up the rest of your body, then rinse well. You may not need to condition every time you shampoo, though, as it may leave your hair too flat and greasy looking. Experiment. There are also leave-in conditioners that you put on damp, towel-dried hair after shampooing. Use these sparingly, as they can irritate your scalp and weigh down your hair, making it look flat. Again, experiment with different brands.

No more tangles. Work out tangles carefully with your fingers while your hair is still wet. Dragging a brush or comb through your hair not only is painful but can cause damage.

Dry carefully. If you like to blow-dry your hair, towel it dry first to remove most of the moisture. Hair experts recommend using medium-to-high heat on a low-speed setting. Keep the dryer at least 6 inches from your scalp, and keep it moving—don't hold it in one place. Turn off the dryer when the top layer of hair is still slightly damp; don't overdry. Ideally, it's best not to use a blow dryer at all, but as most people will attest, no blow dryer equals bad hair day.

Movers and Shavers

Men used to pay barbers to have their faces shaved and their mustaches trimmed—and women didn't talk about how they removed their unwanted hair.

Nowadays, the choice you make about what to do with that body hair that's starting to grow—on your face if you're a guy and on your legs and under your arms if you're a girl—is a matter of personal preference. You can remove it, or you can let it grow.

FOR GUYS

Boys start growing facial hair during puberty, usually around stage 4, after the sex organs are fairly well developed. Look for it between ages 14 and 16, but you could get it at age 13 or age 20. The first hairs usually appear just above the corners of your lips.

Don't expect a big, bushy mustache overnight. You'll get just a few tiny, light, almost unnoticeable hairs first that will gradually get darker and thicker as you get older. Your mustache will grow in from the corners inward. At the same time, you may notice a little hair start to grow just below the center of your lower lip and on your upper cheeks—what eventually will fill in as a beard—and your sideburns may start to come in. Your facial hair probably will be the same color as the hair on your head, but it could vary, too.

Remember, all this will take a while. You may get a full, thick mustache and beard by the time you're 18, or it may not come in completely until you're 10 years past puberty.

Once you notice your facial hair start to come in, you might be anxious to start shaving. Go ahead and try—ask your dad to show you how to use his shaver—but keep in mind that you may not have much hair to cut for now. We'll give you some tips on shaving in the next section.

FOR GIRLS

Your first underarm and leg hairs probably will come in at about the time you start growing pubic hair, around stage 2 or 3. For whatever reason, boys are allowed more social leeway in what they do with their body hair, whereas girls usually feel the need to shave their armpits and legs. You may wish to engage in this depilatory ritual, which is perfectly fine, or you may choose not to shave your underarms, which is OK also—just tell everyone "It's the European look."

Like the guys, however, you may not have much hair to shave at first. Underarm hair usually comes in about two years after your pubic hair starts to grow. The hair on your legs becomes a little darker during puberty, too.

In rare cases, you may notice slightly darker hairs on your upper lip as well that may resemble a faint mustache. This is normal and does not mean you are any less feminine. If you shave this hair, you will create stubble and the hair probably will grow back thicker and even darker. And using chemicals to remove it can burn or scar your skin. The hair is not noticeable to anyone but you. However, if there is enough of it to make you feel uncomfortable, talk to your parents or a doctor.

THE ART OF SHAVING

If you've decided to go the hair-removal route, read on. According to *Consumer Reports,* cartridge razors work better than disposable razors. But cartridges are more expensive, which is probably why they're used by less than half of all people who shave.

If you want to use a cartridge razor, have your dad or mom or another experienced person show you how to use one first. Always start with a fresh, unnicked blade and throw it away at the first sign of pulling or tugging on your skin or hair.

Don't borrow another person's razor. Razors can spread skin diseases such as herpes or warts. Like a toothbrush, this item should be for your own personal use only.

Disposable razors are available in packets at supermarkets or drugstores. These work well and should be thrown away after each use.

Electric shavers cut hair in either a circular or back-and-forth motion. These do a nifty job on hair removal—and you won't risk cutting yourself. However, you may not get as close a shave as you would with a manual razor. Don't press too hard while using an electric shaver, because you can get razor burn. And, of course, keep all electric shavers—and all electrical appliances—away from water.

Some battery-operated razors are waterproof and allow you to shave when your skin is wet. These products will say "fully submersible" or "wet/dry" on them. They're often used by those with sensitive skin.

Hair is easier to cut if it's wet, so take a quick shower first. Some people prefer to shave while they're in the shower. Shaving gel or cream has more lubricants than plain bar soap does, and will help the razor glide over your skin more smoothly. Move the razor in slow, light, gentle strokes. For more effective

THE BALD AND THE BEAUTIFUL

Not every man experiences hair loss, but many do. You won't have to worry about it until you're around 40. But bald can be beautiful. Just ask former basketball star Michael Jordan, talk-show host Montel Williams, and actor John Malkovich—they all *choose* to shave their heads.

removal of underarm hair, shave up and down, not side to side. To avoid sting, wait a little while after shaving to apply deodorant or antiperspirant. If you're a guy, shave your cheeks first, then the sides of your face, then your chin and lip area.

Rinse the blade often while you're shaving to wash off hair and gel buildup. When you're done, rinse yourself with cool water and towel dry. Rinse your blade and shake it dry. Don't wipe it, as this may damage the cutting edge. Finally, sweat can irritate just-shaven skin, so avoid shaving right before you exercise.

Blood, Sweat, and Fears

Little kids don't sweat it—literally—because they perspire only when they've been running around a lot or when it's hot outdoors. Even then, they don't sweat very much.

Puberty changes all that. The hormones that trigger your oil glands send the same message to your sweat glands: "Pump up the volume!"

Around the same time you notice hair growing under your arms, you'll also notice that your underarm perspiration is increasing, creating wet stains on your clothing. In addition, an odor may be present that wasn't there before. The sweat itself is not what smells; it comes in contact with the bacteria on your skin, creating an odor. Your hands and feet also might start to sweat, too, even when you're not nervous or engaged in a physical activity.

Sweating is normal and healthy. It's your body's way of cooling off, just as your dog pants to cool itself off. Still, the thought of giving off an unpleasant odor or having visible stains under your arms can be unsettling whether you're a guy or a girl. Luckily, dealing with this issue is nothing to sweat about. Just follow these tips.

Stay clean. Take a shower or bath daily and after you've worked up a sweat. Wash with plain or antibacterial soap and warm or hot water.

Wear clean clothes. No more living in dirty shorts, T-shirts, or sweats. If you haven't done so already, now is a good time to learn how to operate the washing machine.

Give cotton a try. Natural fabrics such as cotton and wool are more absorbent than synthetic fabrics such as polyester and will keep you cooler. Wearing 100 percent cotton clothing in warm weather will help wick away sweat from your body.

Deodorize. You may want to use a deodorant or an antiperspirant after you bathe or shower. A deodorant is designed to mask or cover body odor; it does not keep you from sweating. An antiperspirant stops perspiration—most of it. Both products come in sprays, creams, sticks, and roll-ons. Experiment to see which one suits you best. Some are marketed toward men, others toward women, but in truth, their ingredients are the same.

THE NATURAL WAY

Some commercial deodorant products contain skin irritants. You might be able to find better products in health-food stores. Look for deodorants that contain green tea extract, which is antibacterial. Splashing rubbing alcohol under your arms is an easy way to reduce bacteria. Caffeine makes your sweat glands secrete more, so avoid coffee and tea.

Keep in mind, though, that deodorants and antiperspirants can stain your clothes over time. Kind of counterproductive when you think about it, isn't it? Usually, daily showering or bathing and wearing clean clothes is enough to do the trick. Besides, not everyone will have a noticeable body odor anyway.

If you decide to deodorize, wait about 10 minutes after your shower or bath. This allows your body to cool off so that the deodorant or antiperspirant "sticks" and doesn't melt off.

The Skinny on Sunscreen

Your skin is the largest organ in your body. The average human body is covered by 14 to 18 square feet of skin.

Skin does much more than hold together your bones and muscles. It manufactures waxes and oils that make you waterproof and protect you from harmful germs and bacteria. It keeps your body fluid in where it belongs. It helps your body get rid of chemicals it doesn't need. It's like a protective suit of armor against all sorts of wear and tear.

The sun is one of your skin's worst enemies. Sunlight contains invisible ultraviolet (UV) rays that can burn your skin and cause wrinkles, dark spots (also called sunspots), blotches, and growths to appear. The chemical melanin in your skin is the body's first defense against UV rays. Melanin absorbs the sun's rays and causes your skin to tan. The darker your skin, the more melanin it contains. That's why light-skinned people are less protected against sunburn than those who are dark skinned. Even if your skin is black or brown, though, you can still burn.

> ## PUCKER UP!
>
> Why does the skin on your palms and the soles of your feet wrinkle after a shower or a swim? The skin here is different than the skin elsewhere on your body. It is thicker and harder for protection because you use your hands and feet so often. It swells as it absorbs water, causing it to expand and look wrinkled.

PLAYING IT SAFE

In recent years, the dangers of skin cancer have received increased publicity—and with good reason. Doctors once thought skin cancer appeared only in older people, but it has now been found in people in their 20s.

Skin cancer is the most common type of cancer in the United States. Prolonged sun damage is the primary cause, although family history also plays a factor. Again, fair-skinned people are more prone to skin cancer than African-Americans or dark-skinned people.

What's unique about your skin is that it "stores" sun damage, meaning the sunburn you got as a kid will be with you forever. Skin cancer can take 10 to 20 years to develop, so it's important to take precautions now.

Put on sunscreen or sunblock whenever you're going to be out in the sun for an extended period of time, say 20 to 30 minutes or more. (Sunscreen absorbs and filters UV rays; sunblock blocks out all the rays and provides better protection.) Reapply it often, because it can get rubbed off or washed off by sweat or water. If you're fair skinned, it's a good idea to put on sunscreen every day whether or not you're going to be in the sun for a long time. Check with your doctor.

Sunscreens and sunblocks filter out those damaging UV rays. They are rated by their sun protection factor (SPF) followed by a number. If the number is 4, the product provides 4 times the protection you would get if you didn't use a sunscreen. Don't be deceived, though. It all depends on how long it takes you to burn. If you burn in just 10 minutes, an SPF of 4 will not do you much good. Use a product with an SPF rating of at least 15, whether you burn easily or not.

Apply the sunscreen to every part of your body that's exposed to the sun. Don't forget the back of your neck; a lot of people neglect to cover this sensitive area. For the best protection, apply at least 15 minutes before going outdoors. Be certain to follow the directions on the container.

Choose a waterproof sunblock if you're going swimming or playing a sport where you'll sweat a lot, and keep reapplying it. "Waterproof" means it will *resist* being washed or sweated off, but that doesn't mean all of it will stay on the whole time you're out.

Worried about aggravating your acne? Again, look for oil-free or noncomedogenic sunscreen products. These won't clog your pores or cause pimples.

The Eyes Have It

Your eyes are just as sensitive to sun damage as your skin. In fact, one day in strong sunlight can burn your corneas (the clear, outermost layer of your eyes). Such burns can cause cataracts, a clouding of the eye's lens, and result in blindness.

Protect your eyes by getting into the habit of wearing sunglasses. Not all sunglasses are sun safe, however. Buy only glasses that are labeled "100 percent UV protection."

CHAPTER 5

That Three-Letter Word

My friends talk about sex a lot. I just listen most of the time because they sound so experienced and I'm not at all. Sometimes I feel like I should have sex just so I can know what it's like.

—Jennifer, age 13

Now we come to everyone's favorite three-letter subject, and it's not Art.

You may already know something about sex because you've had discussions with your friends, or you've been sat down to have "The Talk" with one or both of your parents. Or maybe you tune in to Adam and Dr. Drew on *Loveline* regularly. (C'mon, admit it.)

You might be thinking about sex a lot, or just curious about it. Then again, having sex may be the *last* thing on your mind right now. Take heart, you're neither a sex addict nor a prude; you're normal. But you probably don't know everything you'd like to know, or think you'd like to know, about that three-letter word.

The word *sex* is confusing because it has so many different meanings in our culture. The textbook definition is the physical differences between men's and women's bodies, most obviously the sex organs. The word also is used to describe having sex. We also say that we have "sexual feelings," which can mean we are sexually attracted to another person, or we are thinking about our sex organs, or we are thinking about sexual pleasure.

But sex is more than just the "facts of life"—that is, how babies are made. And it's more than just "doing the nasty," or whatever other slang term you may have heard. It's not just the physical act. Your emotional maturity, your attitude toward the opposite sex (and your own sex for that matter), your outlook on your own changing body and feelings—all play a factor. In turn, your sexuality—the quality, both physical and emotional, of your maleness or femaleness—shapes how others relate to you and how you feel about yourself.

A Head Case

Despite what you've heard and read about all the tools to good sex—everything from vibrators to Viagra—sex begins in your head. Again, it's outlook, attitude, and, above all, knowledge and education that are the keys to a healthy sexuality. The more you know, the better you'll be prepared to make important decisions when it comes to sex, or any other important life issues for that matter. So when they say that size matters, they're right—the size of your brain, that is.

Teresa Ann Donnelly Weyer, B.S., is a Southern California health educator. She developed a course in family health and sex education that is used in school districts throughout the state. At the beginning of each year, she asks students in her classes at Highland High School in Palmdale, California, to write down and submit questions about sex. The most frequently asked questions are found in the list below. These and other issues are addressed in the text that follows.

✿ Just what *is* sexual intercourse?

✿ How does birth control work?

✿ Do boys and girls think differently about having sex?

❀ What's the difference between sex and love?

❀ Can a girl get pregnant the first time she has sex?

❀ I've been masturbating like I'm trying to break a world record or something. Am I normal?

❀ A lot of kids at school say they're "doing it" or hooking up. Is there anything wrong with me if I'm not?

❀ What is "safe sex"?

❀ What are STDs, and how do you get them?

Staying the Course

When a man inserts his penis into a woman's vagina, they are having sexual intercourse. That's the technical definition. But as is often the case, what makes intercourse pleasurable are the feelings, intimacy, and emotions that are felt before, during, and after the act.

You may be wondering how a guy could even get his penis inside a girl, or why he would even want to. When a man and a woman care deeply for each other, they may choose to show their love by having sex. They may begin by holding, kissing, and fondling each other. If the woman becomes aroused, her clitoris swells with blood, and her vagina becomes wet with secretions that make it easier for the penis to slip inside. If the man becomes aroused, his penis swells with blood and hardens.

When both partners are ready, the man enters the woman's vagina and moves his penis rhythmically back and forth, increasing the pressure and causing him to become more aroused. The woman can increase her arousal by rubbing her clitoris with her finger, or asking the man to do so. The heart beats more rapidly and breathing becomes heavier in both partners.

At the peak of sexual pleasure, each partner will *orgasm,* also called "come" or "climax." The man and woman may not necessarily orgasm at the same time, however.

When a man orgasms, muscles in the penis and around the prostate gland contract, and he ejaculates semen that contains sperm. The semen comes out in a few spurts that happen within a second or two of each other.

When a woman orgasms, she experiences the same release of built-up energy that a man does, along with a sensation that sort of flows over her body in waves. She also may feel her clitoris pulse and the muscles of her uterus contract. In some women, the glands may produce a gush of fluid, but this is not the same as a guy's ejaculation.

You Mean It's Not Like Kate and Leonardo in Titanic?

Now you have a *clinical* understanding of what sexual intercourse is, but unless you also have an emotional attachment to your partner and feel comfortable with your own body, the level of pleasure and enjoyment may not necessarily be what you expect—or expected—the first time you have sex. We're not trying to scare you off by saying sex is bad, because it's not. We just want you to know that it's not like you see in the movies or read in those bodice-rippers (you know, romance novels). Those are pure fantasy.

Save Me an Egg

Semen contains millions of sperm. A normal ejaculation holds more than 300 million sperm. The sperm can be seen only under a microscope and are even tinier than a woman's ovum, which is about the size of the tip of a sharpened pencil; all the sperm could fit on the head of a pin.

Each sperm has three parts:

1. The head, which contains the genetic material that the man contributes to making a baby.

2. The middle section, which gives the sperm the energy to move.

3. The tail, which propels the sperm forward.

Once the sperm are in the vagina after ejaculation and an egg happens to be present, they immediately swim in the direction of the egg. If no ovum is present, the sperm will swim erratically and eventually die off. (Sperm can survive in a woman's body for only about 48 hours.)

It may take up to a few days for the sperm to find their way to the fallopian tube, where they

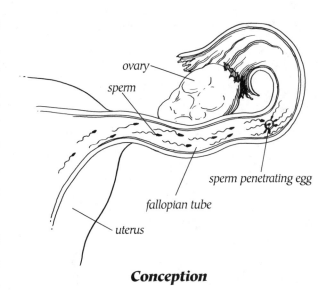

ovary

sperm

sperm penetrating egg

fallopian tube

uterus

Conception

meet the ovum. It's not an easy journey. Some sperm die when exposed to air after the penis is withdrawn from the vagina. Some are killed off after passing through the cervical mucus. Others may get "lost" and swim the wrong way. Still others may be slow swimmers and simply die of "old age."

The sperm that reach their goal surround the ovum. As soon as one burrows its way into the egg and fertilizes it, the egg "locks out" the rest of the swimmers and prevents them from penetrating. The fertilized ovum then makes it way down into the uterus, where it imbeds itself in the endometrium—the lining that builds up in the wall of the uterus—and proceeds to grow into a baby. Because the egg has been implanted, the endometrium is not shed and passed out of the body. The woman does not have a period, which can be one sign that she is pregnant. Some women may have slight bleeding or spotting, however, which may be mistaken for a period.

A man can produce sperm at just about any time, and well into his senior years. That's why celebrities such as Warren Beatty and Tony Randall have fathered children in their 60s and 70s. Women, however, are born with a set number of eggs, and release one egg—ovulate—about once a month until they stop having periods (menopause), which usually happens between the ages of 45 and 50.

Myth #1: A girl can't get pregnant the first time she has sex.

Fact: Ten percent of all teen pregnancies occur the first month a girl starts having sex. Fifty percent occur in the first six months!

Myth #2: A girl can't get pregnant if she has sex in a swimming pool, or in a hot tub, because the heat will kill the sperm.

Fact: Being in water won't "wash out" the sperm, and although heat may reduce sperm production in a guy over a period of time, remember, there are *millions and millions* of those little swimmers.

Myth #3: A girl can't get pregnant if she has sex while she is having her period.

Fact: It's rare, but you *can* have a short cycle and ovulate right on the heels of your last period.

It's plain and simple: Whenever a boy and a girl have sexual intercourse, a pregnancy can occur.

Birth Control

Pregnancy is most likely to occur when a couple has unprotected sex up to five days before the woman ovulates. Because teen girls—and even some adult women—have irregular periods, it is almost impossible to know exactly when she will ovulate.

That's why birth control is so important if you and your partner have decided to have sex and do not want to become pregnant. Also called *contraception*, birth control consists of several methods used to prevent pregnancy.

Most methods work in one of three ways:

1. Prevent the sperm from reaching the egg and fertilizing it.

2. Prevent the woman from ovulating.

3. Prevent a fertilized egg from growing in the uterus.

Condoms

Also called a *rubber* or *prophylactic,* a condom is a tube of polyurethane or latex that is unrolled onto an erect penis. A receptacle at the end traps semen and prevents it from entering the vagina. Some condoms contain a spermicide, a chemical that kills sperm. They come in a variety of styles and textures, from ribbed to micro-thin, intended to provide different sensations. Condoms are available at any drugstore or supermarket.

If you use a condom, it will slip on easier and feel more sensitive if you lubricate the penis, particularly the head. Water-based lubricants such as K-Y Jelly work better than oil-based lubricants, which break down latex and make the condom less effective. *Never* reuse a condom. (As if you would want to.)

Condoms are the only birth control method for men—so far. The remaining methods are designed to be used by women.

Birth control pills

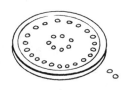

Also called *oral contraceptives* or simply *"the pill,"* birth control pills contain the hormones estrogen and progesterone, or progesterone only. To be most effective, they must be taken every day at about the same time.

Basically, the pill works by preventing a girl from ovulating. It is also used for other gynecological conditions, not just as a contraceptive. The pill may be prescribed to reduce the amount of menstrual flow, to alleviate severe cramping, and to establish more regular cycles. Aside from abstinence (not engaging in any sex), the pill—when used correctly—is one of the most effective forms of birth control (see the chart on page 82).

The pill, however, has side effects, including possible weight gain, mood swings, and acne. More severe but rare side effects are blood clots, stroke, and heart attack. Each brand or type of pill can have its own effects on each girl. They're available only by visiting a clinic or your gynecologist. Talk with your gynecologist about what's best for you.

Norplant

Norplant is a device that contains hormones similar to those found in birth control pills. Small capsules are implanted under the skin, and a constant low dose of hor-mone is released and absorbed into the body. Depending on the type, Norplant lasts from three to five years. See a doctor if you're interested in Norplant.

IUDs

An intrauterine device (IUD) is placed inside the uterus during minor surgery. This copper device keeps a fertilized egg from implanting in the uterine wall. IUDs are not recommended for teens because of their high complication rate. They can cause severe pelvic infections, which may make it hard to get pregnant in the future.

Diaphragms

A diaphragm is a soft, rubberlike device that is shaped like a half sphere. The woman fills it with spermicide, then inserts it into the vagina before intercourse. The diaphragm must be inserted deep enough so that it covers the cervix and blocks out sperm. It must be left in for at least 8 hours after intercourse. It can then be removed, washed, and reused. To get a diaphragm, you must visit a gynecologist, who will fit one to your body.

Cervical caps

A cervical cap is similar to but smaller than a diaphragm and is used in the same way. This device also must be fitted by a gynecologist.

Contraceptive sponges

The sponge is soft and shaped like a small doughnut with an indentation instead of a hole. It is used like a diaphragm or cervical cap, except it already contains spermicide, which makes it more convenient to use than the other two methods. The sponge is no longer available, but at press time there were plans to bring it back on the market. Keep an eye out.

Female condoms

A recent addition to the contraceptive family, the female condom is a large pouch made of polyurethane or latex that is inserted into the vagina before intercourse, creating a "sleeve" for the penis to fit into and preventing sperm from entering the vagina. Female condoms are available at specialty stores (those that sell contraceptives and other sex-related items) and some drugstores.

He Said, She Said

Although some boys and girls may be raised *equally*, they're not raised *identically*. That's probably why each looks at sex differently. Some girls have a more romantic view of sexual relationships; warmth, intimacy, caring, and tenderness are more important to them. Some guys, on the other hand, see sexual relationships as short-term physical experiences that may or may not involve romantic feelings.

But before you lump all guys together as insensitive pigs, or all girls together as emotional saps, keep in mind that there are some guys who appreciate tenderness, and some girls who prefer the physical aspects over all the flowers and hand-holding. Still others—perhaps including you—probably fall somewhere in between.

One outlook is not necessarily better than the other. But when all this relationship stuff is new to you, it helps to understand where the opposite sex is coming from. Girls and guys are, well, wired differently, to put it in a nutshell. This knowledge may not prevent you from being hurt or confused when a relationship ends or is not going as well as you'd like, but it will help you deal with it and learn from it.

IF YOU REALLY LOVED ME...

One of the most common misunderstandings between boys and girls—and you've probably seen it among your friends, or maybe in a relationship you recently had—is confusing sexual feelings with love. If you love someone, you may think you have to have sex with that person, for whatever reason: to prove your love, to keep him or her from leaving, to show how grown-up you are.

That is so *not* true. You can love someone, enjoy his or her company, and share common interests without having sex and taking on the risks that come with having a sexual relationship. As a teen—or as an adult, for that matter—you should never let anyone talk you into doing something you don't feel comfortable doing.

But say you're not uncomfortable, and you really do want to have sex with your special someone, and the feeling is mutual. In that case, you really need to think things through.

First, are you ready to face the consequences—and the responsibilities—if you get pregnant? Second, are you aware of the risks of contracting a sexually transmitted disease (STD)? (Read the section on STDs starting on page 78.) Third, when you engage in sexual intercourse, you are exposing yourself physically, mentally, and emotionally. Sexual experiences tend to be safer, and more satisfying, when they are shared with someone you can

ONE BIRTH CONTROL METHOD THAT DOESN'T WORK

Withdrawal (pulling the penis out of the vagina before you come) is the most ineffective form of birth control. When a boy becomes sexually aroused, some seminal fluid—filled with sperm—comes out of the penis. This happens way before ejaculation, while the penis is still inside the vagina.

trust, someone who is committed to you, someone you can show your best and worst sides to. Are you really ready to deal with this at this time, with this person?

Think of what you want to accomplish in school and in life. You have many years ahead of you to explore and answer all the questions you have. Make the decision that's wisest and best for you.

Let's be real: Some of you will decide to go ahead and have sex. If so, we can't emphasize this enough: *Use protection.*

Masturbation

Touching or stroking your genitals to give your-self a pleasurable feeling—with or without cli-maxing—is called masturbation or masturbating. Lots of people—many more than will probably admit—masturbate at some point in their lives. Both guys and girls do it. It's perfectly normal if you do—and perfectly normal if you don't.

Girls usually masturbate by rubbing their clitoris with their fingers. Their vulva and vagina may become wet as they become aroused. Some women may use a battery-operated device called a vibrator to manipulate

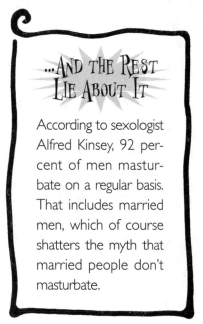

...AND THE REST LIE ABOUT IT

According to sexologist Alfred Kinsey, 92 percent of men masturbate on a regular basis. That includes married men, which of course shatters the myth that married people don't masturbate.

the clitoris or insert into the vagina. Whenever you hear about masturbation it's usually in reference to guys, but it's perfectly acceptable for girls to explore and talk about their bodies as well, so don't feel weird if you're a girl and you're mas-turbating. The number of women who masturbate is a lot higher than you think.

Boys may begin masturbating before puberty, but they won't ejaculate until their testicles start to make sperm, which doesn't happen until they hit puberty. The first ejaculation usually occurs around age 13 or 14, but it could happen ear-lier or later. Some guys masturbate several times a day, some a couple of times a week. Wherever you fall in the spectrum is normal for you.

Contrary to the myths and stories that still abound to this day, masturbation is not "bad" or harmful in any way. In the old days, people believed masturbation caused you to go blind, or insane, or hair to grow on the palms of your hands. Nowadays masturbation is considered normal, even though it still isn't talked about much in public. Besides relieving sexual tension and energy, masturbating can help you become comfortable with your body and learn what makes it feel good. The idea is, whenever you do decide to have sex, you will be able to tell your partner what areas to touch to bring you the greatest pleasure.

Is Everyone "Doing It"?

It may seem to you that everyone is hooking up except you. But rest assured that not everyone is having or has had sex. In fact, more teens probably are *not* doing it than are. Some may just be bragging or exaggerating to look cool or fit in. Some may have thought they went "all the way" when they really didn't. In reality, most teens as just as inexperienced as you are when it comes to sex.

> ### DOUBLE DUTY
>
> No matter which type of birth control you use, back it up with a latex condom. This practice not only will give you an added barrier against those anxious little sperm, but also will provide protection against contracting an STD.

Sexually Transmitted Diseases

Before you say yes to having sex, there are some important facts you should know. Each year millions of teens and adults contract a sexually transmitted disease (STD). Of course, the only sure way not to get an STD is not to have sex. Even if you aren't sexually active, you should be aware of what STDs are and what they do.

AIDS

Acquired immune deficiency syndrome, more commonly known as AIDS, is a disease caused by the human immunodeficiency virus, or HIV. HIV attacks the body's immune system, which is its built-in defense mechanism against disease. The body is left with no protection against even common diseases, like a cold or flu, that can be easily fought off if you're healthy. There are treatments but no cures for AIDS, and even though new vaccines are currently being tested, a full-blown case of AIDS usually ends in death.

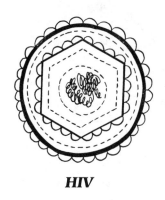

HIV

You can acquire HIV by coming into contact with the bodily fluids of an already infected person. HIV is transmitted through sexual intercourse, sharing hypodermic needles, and receiving a blood transfusion from an infected person. A pregnant woman with HIV can pass the virus on to her baby either in the womb or through her breast milk.

Hepatitis B

A highly infectious disease that attacks the liver, hepatitis B, commonly called *hep B*, is spread by sexual contact or contact with infected blood or bodily fluids.

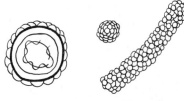

3 Different Forms of Hepatitis B Virus

About 300,000 cases of hep B are discovered each year, most of them among young people. Many of those who are infected show no symptoms until the disease has progressed and complications set in. Among the symptoms are jaundice (a yellowing of the skin and eyes), dark-colored urine, nausea, and fatigue. Hep B has no cure. Treatment consists of bed rest along with a high-protein diet to repair damaged cells, and a high-carbohydrate diet to protect the liver. To help combat the spread of the disease, most infants are vaccinated shortly after birth.

Genital herpes

Forty million people in the United States have genital herpes, and as many as 500,000 new cases are diagnosed each year. Caused by a virus, this disease

Herpes Virus

results in painful blisters and sometimes open sores in the genital area or around the mouth. The virus is transmitted through sexual contact. Pregnant women can pass genital herpes to their babies while givng birth. Once infected, there is no cure. Certain drugs can reduce the frequency and length of the blister outbreaks.

Genital warts

Genital warts are brought on by the human papilloma virus (HPV). They appear in and around the sex organs and can be flat, raised, single or multiple, small or large, and can erupt in clusters. The warts are spread by skin-to-skin contact during sex. Treatment includes creams or drugs; sometimes the warts are frozen off or removed with a laser, but even after treatment they may come back. Approximately 750,000 Americans are infected each year.

Human Papilloma Virus

Chlamydia

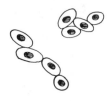

Chlamydia

Chlamydia is difficult to detect until painful complications occur. Women may experience itching or burning in their genitals and a vaginal discharge, while men may have pain while urinating. Treatment is with antibiotics. If chlamydia is left untreated, it can lead to pelvic inflammatory disease (PID) in women, which in some cases can cause sterility and, even worse, death.

Gonorrhea

Often called "the clap," gonorrhea is common among sexually active teens. In females, it frequently goes undetected until the disease moves upward into the uterus, fallopian tubes, and ovaries, where, like chlamydia, it can cause PID. In males,

Gonorrhea

symptoms include a discharge from the penis and a burning sensation during urination. Gonorrhea can be treated with antibiotics.

Syphilis

Symptoms of this STD are painless sores on the genitals or the mouth. Before the discovery of antibiotics, syphilis attacked the heart and brain, causing blindness and death. Now, it is diagnosed through a blood test and treated with antibiotics.

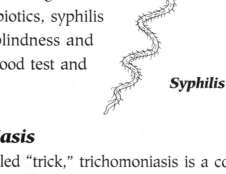

Syphilis

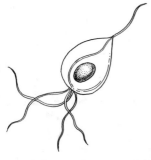

Trichomoniasis

Trichomoniasis

Sometimes called "trick," trichomoniasis is a common cause of irritation or inflammation of the vagina. Its symptoms are pain while urinating and a foul-smelling discharge from the vagina. Men who are infected often do not show symptoms and can unknowingly pass on the disease to their sex partners. Treatment is with antibiotics.

Pubic lice

Pubic lice, also called "crabs," are tiny, blood-sucking insects that cause itching and irritation. Although technically not a disease, lice are spread through sexual contact. They are not life threatening, but they're no picnic, either. To get rid of pubic lice, you must use a special lotion, wash your clothes and sheets in ultrahot water, and put them in sealed plastic bags for at least two weeks to kill the insects. Definitely not anyone's idea of fun. (Just *try* finding bags big enough.)

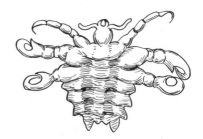

Pubic Louse

Safe Sex

Safe sex involves using a condom—properly, mind you—to protect both parties from giving or contracting an STD. It's also the term used to protect against pregnancy. In reality, though, "safe sex" is misleading. If you're having sex, you can never be 100 percent safe from either getting pregnant or getting an STD.

The chart below illustrates the effectiveness of the various methods of birth control we've discussed in this chapter. As you will see, some methods are more effective than others for preventing pregnancy and the transmission of STDs.

A GOOD BACKUP PLAN

Oral contraceptives, Norplant, and IUDs are the most effective methods of birth control, but they provide no—repeat, no—protection against STDs. If you are on the pill or using any of these methods, always use a condom as a backup during sex.

Method	Effectiveness Against STDs[1]	Percentage of Women Who Got Pregnant with This Method[2]	Visit to a Doctor Necessary?
Condom	Very good	3 to 12	No
Female condom	Very good	5 to 21	No
Spermicide only	Fair	6 to 21	No
Diaphragm	Fair	6 to 18	Yes
Contraceptive sponge	Fair	9 to 36	No
Cervical cap	Fair	9 to 36	Yes
The pill	None	0.1 to 3	Yes
Norplant	None	<1	Yes
IUD	None	0.1 to 2	Yes

[1] If used correctly every time the couple has intercourse.
[2] Percentages represent failure rate in 100 women during the first year of use.

CHAPTER 6

I Second That Emotion

Sometimes I get so upset and confused I could just scream. One minute I feel great, and the next I feel awful. I don't know why, and that just gets me more upset. Everyone else seems to be normal except me. Am I a total space case?

—Roxanne, age 13½

In this period in your life, your emotions—how you feel—are changing as fast as your body, perhaps even faster.

It's more than just feeling like you're on an emotional roller coaster, as the cliché goes. It's more like the space shuttle flying through a meteor shower. Something sets you off, and suddenly you're uptight and angry, or you're laughing uncontrollably and your friends are saying, "What's up with you?" Sometimes you feel so funky you don't even want to get out of bed, and the next minute you want to shout to the whole world, "Bring it on!"

Psychologist Andrea Schalman, Ph.D., M.F.C.C. (that's short for marriage, family, and child counselor), says kids have lots of questions about their feelings during puberty. In her private practice in Manhattan Beach, California, she talks to teens just like you.

Here are some questions Dr. Schalman's clients frequently ask her.

✿ Sometimes my parents make me so mad! At other times I feel so much love and appreciation for them. Am I weird or what?

✿ I cry over the stupidest things, like a movie about animals, or when I get angry about something or at someone. Is this normal?

✿ Is it nerdy to want to talk to someone—besides my parents—about how I feel about things? Since their divorce when I was 8, I feel like I'm all alone, even though I have stepsisters and a couple of half brothers.

✿ All these school shootings across the country have me scared. What if something like that happened at my school?

✿ I've gotten into trouble at school and my parents are major ticked-off. I think running away would solve my problems since no one understands how I feel. Can a 14-year-old start a life on her own?

✿ My best friend has always been the guy next door. Now I get nervous whenever I'm around him. I think I have a crush on him. What should I do?

✿ I feel stressed out a lot, but everyone says only adults get stressed. Is this true?

Got Those Moody Blues?

Welcome to Pubertyland, where you feel up one day and down the next, where someone can be your best friend one day, and your worst enemy a couple days later.

During your stay, not only can your friendships shift, but your emotions can, too. For instance, your sister or brother can be really obnoxious to you in the morning and it won't bother you a bit—but that same afternoon a little comment from someone else makes your blood boil or your tears flow. Or, you're dreaming about going off to college and being independent, and the next day you just want to cuddle up with your favorite teddy. Or, that girl next to you in class suddenly got a whole lot cuter.

Hey, get with the program. Everyone visits Pubertyland once in their lifetime.

Part of the reason that your emotions seem out of kilter is that you're adjusting to the hormonal changes taking place in your body. Those same hormones that trigger off physical changes also have a lot to do with how and what you're feeling.

Also, there's a lot of new stuff going on in your life. You're meeting new people and trying to make new friends—maybe even going to a new school— and your sense of identity (who you are) is changing, too. You're no longer just your parents' child, you're a person who is learning how to make your own decisions.

All these changes can be confusing—but being confused is a normal state of mind for a teen. You've got all these issues on your plate to deal with. Well, so does everyone else—teen or grown-up, celebrity or regular joe, prom queen or class nerd, teacher or student. If you take a look around, you'll always find someone worse off than you.

When life is getting you down, try the following Blues Beaters:

❀ Get out of the house and MOVE! Working out produces a hormone called beta-endorphin, which helps improve your mood.

❀ Cry if you feel like it! Shedding tears releases tension and actually makes you feel happier.

Parents Just Don't Understand

When you were a kid, you got along great with your parents. But now that you're a teen, things have changed—maybe a lot, maybe a little.

During your childhood, you didn't have much say in a lot of things. You ate what was put on your plate, you used the shampoo that was in the bathroom, you went to bed when you were told.

Now, you probably want to pick your own shampoo, go to bed when you want, eat foods your parents think are unhealthy (or downright gross!), and hang out with friends who are pierced and other people your parents may not be crazy about, but you don't see anything wrong with them.

You're asserting your independence, but your parents are still asserting their control because they are still primarily responsible for you. This can and does cause conflict. Clashes with parents are a fact of life for most teens.

The good news is that in time, the power struggle will end. You'll learn the art of compromise, and your parents will learn to let go.

Until then, it's important to keep your mind and the lines of communication open when it comes to the parental units. In other words, you've got to train them.

For starters, put yourself in their shoes. Your parents spent many years raising you as a child, and still see you that way. They need time to adjust to the "new" you. And they really are concerned about you and where you're headed in life.

Talk with your parents and explain your opinions calmly. A helpful method is to use "I feel…" statements instead of "You always…" accusations. Your parents may not always agree with your point of view, but they probably will listen and just might compromise. They were once teenagers, too, and probably had a lot of the same feelings you do. If you start getting angry, take a deep breath and check your temper. Losing it is a sure way to break down those lines of communication.

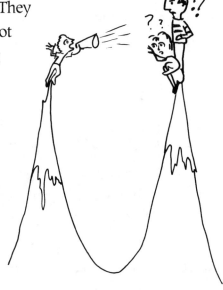

Also, keep in mind that no matter how old you get, you will always be your parents' child, someone they want to protect and keep safe. You know, your grandparents still feel protective toward your parents no matter how old they are.

It's Not Bad to Be Sad

Just a few years ago, when you were a wee lad or lass, that scene in *Bambi* where his mother dies didn't make you shed one tear. Instead, you thought Thumper was way cool. But if you watched that movie now, that scene might leave you a blubbering mass of human flesh. What gives?

Sadness is a normal emotion, and one that teens feel a lot. You'll probably find that as you progress through puberty and your body adjusts to the hormones that are flooding through your system, you'll feel sad less often.

DEALING WITH DEPRESSION

When they're down in the dumps, many people say "I'm so depressed." It's OK to feel sad and negative occasionally in response to a particular event, such as a poor grade on an exam or the death of someone close. But if feelings of hopelessness and a loss of interest in life in general are brought on without any apparent cause and do not go away, it may be a sign of *clinical depression*. Depression is a psychiatric disorder that is not the same as just feeling sad or unhappy. It can happen to anyone. Even teens who are totally upbeat most of their lives can become depressed.

Although experts do not know what causes depression, research suggests that depression may be hereditary. If one of your family members has a history of depression, you may be at a higher risk for it yourself—but it doesn't mean you will experience it for sure.

Depression is accompanied by changes in a person's brain. The brain contains chemicals called neurotransmitters whose job is to send messages between nerve cells and to regulate your mood. When not enough mood-regulating messages are sent, the result can be depression.

Doctors look for certain signs to determine whether a person is depressed. Any major depression MUST be treated by a psychologist or psychiatrist. A teen may be diagnosed as severely depressed if he or she shows five or more of the following symptoms for more than two weeks:

- ✿ A sad mood that continues and is brought on for no apparent reason.

- ✿ Not enjoying things that once made the person happy.

- ✿ Feeling tired all the time.

- ✿ Feeling angry, anxious, or annoyed all the time.

- ✿ Inability to concentrate.

- ✿ Sudden weight loss or gain.

- ✿ Changes in sleep habits (can't fall asleep, can't get up in the morning, keep waking up during the night).

- ✿ Aches and pains that have no physical cause but don't go away.

- ✿ Loss of interest in life right now or in the future.

- ✿ Thoughts of death or suicide.

Some teens may experience a milder form of depression called *dysthymia*. This disorder can last for two or more years and can make you feel unhappy and even scared and isolated. These are some symptoms of dysthymia:

- ✿ Inability to sleep or sleeping too much.

- ✿ Feeling tired all the time for no reason.

- ✿ Not being able to concentrate or make a decision.

- ✿ Feelings of hopelessness.

- ✿ Feelings of worthlessness or low self-esteem.

The good news is that dysthymia can be successfully treated, so it's important for anyone who has even this mild form of depression to see a doctor.

Could It Happen Here?

School violence, like the tragic shootings at Columbine in 1999 and other schools in several communities across America, might have you in a whirlwind of emotions, from scared to angry to confused to sad.

But let's put things in perspective. Despite all the intense media coverage you have seen, keep in mind what you *don't* see: that there are thousands of *other* schools across the United States where no such violence has occurred or will occur.

Schools actually are very safe environments. But if you still feel that your school isn't a safe place, or that a certain student's words or actions are causing you concern, talk your fears over with your parents, and then with your teacher or school counselor. This may help alleviate your fears.

Learn to trust your feelings, too. If you think a classmate or even a friend is capable of being violent, tell an adult you can trust. And always report *immediately* anyone who brings a weapon to school.

Stay Frosty

Everybody gets angry. Anger is a totally normal emotion. You might get angry when someone makes fun of you or accuses you of doing something you haven't done.

It's how you deal with your anger that's important. You can choose to keep it buried inside, but it's much healthier to learn how to safely blow off steam.

First, keep your cool. You may feel like hitting that creep who's been dogging you, but you shouldn't. You might say, "Well, punching him out would sure make me feel better," but would it really? Even if it did, the feeling lasts only a minute or two. Instead, think about the consequences and the long-term effects of your behavior before you haul off and wallop someone. Responding with violence can only make the situation worse.

People have different ways of dealing with their anger. Some just walk away and don't say a thing. That's OK. Others yell or scream. That's OK, too, as long as it doesn't get out of hand. Still others find that cracking a joke or finding the humor in a situation reduces the tension.

– COOL IT –
HOTHEAD!

Guys and girls tend to deal with their anger differently. For some reason, in our society it's acceptable for a guy to show anger ("I'm so mad I'm about to explode!") but not any other emotions. That's why some boys seem to lose their cool but keep their other feelings bottled up, which just causes more stress, which in turn can lead to more frustration and anger.

Girls, on the other hand, are "socialized" into thinking it's unfeminine to blow their top ("I can't let anyone see how angry I am"). But when they express other feelings, they're often called "too emotional."

Fortunately, we are starting to break down these barriers. Guys are learning how to control their anger while being encouraged to express other emotions. And we're starting to realize that girls often can handle their emotions well because they're more in touch with them.

When you get angry, take a time-out and try to figure out what exactly is bothering you and why. If it's not something you can control—like some idiot who teases you—there's no point getting upset about it.

Again, talking about your feelings helps you sort out your thoughts so you can deal with your anger. Grab a friend, parent, or other trusted person and get her or his perspective on the issue. You can also try one of these Anger Beaters:

✿ Punch out a pillow.

✿ Count to 50 slowly. Don't laugh! It helps you calm down and gain control.

✿ Go for a run or a walk, kick a soccer ball around, or go in-line skating; just getting some fresh air will help clear your head.

✿ Listen to some music.

✿ Jump up and down or stamp your feet. This will help release the tension.

✿ Think about something you like to do or someone you really love.

Don't Be a Runaway

Running away is one of the most dangerous things a teen can do. Each year 1.3 million kids run away, and 5,000 of them will die from assault, illness, or suicide.

You may think life on the streets is glamorous and fun because you can do what you want when you want. Time for a reality check. Living on the streets is downright deadly. People may not be who you think they are, and many teens become sick from malnutrition and fall into drugs and prostitution.

If you know someone who has talked about running away—or if you're thinking of running away yourself—call the National Runaway Hotline at 1-800-621-4000. It's open 24 hours a day and offers help to all potential runaways.

Stressed to the Max

Many adults, who often are dealing with their own stress, forget that stress happens to teens, too. Stress is that feeling you get when a big exam is approaching, or when you're psyching yourself up to ask someone out, or when you're upset after having a fight with your brother or sister.

There is also good stress, too—the kind you feel when you're on vacation, or when your team won the game, or when you're on a date with a special someone. Stress also can be caused by environmental factors that are not in our control, such as air pollution, city noise, and traffic jams.

Stress, good or bad, pumps up the volume on our hormones and kicks our body into temporary overdrive. The sensation you feel is the "fight-or-flight reaction" that occurs when you sense danger. Your heart pumps faster, your blood pressure rises, and you feel a rush of energy, called the adrenaline rush. Of course, being on vacation does not mean you are literally "in danger"; the "danger" can be any type of stressor, positive or negative. This kind of stress usually lasts for just a short while.

Chronic stress, however, is much less intense but can last for days, weeks, or even months. Chronic stress can leave you feeling tired and sick. It can be caused by doing more than you can handle—for instance, having so many activities on your plate that you don't have any downtime. Sometimes chronic stress happens in response to an event you have no control over—for example, if your parents are going through a divorce.

Here are some of the symptoms of chronic stress:

* Headache or stomachache.
* Diarrhea, upset stomach, or indigestion.
* Eating too little or too much.
* Feeling anxious (a fluttery feeling in the pit of your stomach).
* Excessive crying.
* Getting frustrated over things that usually never bother you.
* Getting angry a lot.
* Wanting to be alone more than usual.
* Being unable to sleep.

To help combat stress, try these Stress Beaters:

* Exercise regularly. A run or a fast walk, or playing a game of tennis, will actually reduce your level of stress. Exercise has a calming effect on jangled nerves and tense muscles.

* Get together with your friends and do something you all enjoy. Compare notes—some of them may be feeling stressed out, too.

* Sign up for a yoga class. People who practice yoga claim they feel calmer, less tense, and less stressed because of its beneficial effects.

✿ Do less, not more. If you're already feeling stressed, it's not a good idea to add yet another activity to your roster. Better yet, eliminate one or more of your current activities. Your body and mind will thank you.

✿ If you are experiencing extreme stress—in other words, you're stuck in over-drive and feel exhausted and unable to cope—find a trusted adult to talk with: your mom or dad, your doctor, a favorite teacher or counselor, or your minister, priest, or rabbi.

Talk Is Good

Do you put a cork on your feelings? Are there things you'd like to say or questions you'd like answered? Try the gift of gab.

Talking to someone who's a great listener—if not your parents, then a friend, brother or sister, teacher, coach, counselor, or a leader in your church, synagogue, or wherever you go for religious services—can be good medicine.

It's no longer cool to be the strong, silent type. Teens and adults need to talk more to stay healthy and happy. If you can't find a person to talk with "in person," pick up the phone and call one of the hotlines listed in the back of this book. People who operate the hotlines are professionally trained and truly want to help. They'll listen to your problems and direct you to other people who can provide further assistance.

CHAPTER 7

*B*ody Buildups

All of a sudden I feel hungry all the time. When I'm in the car with my parents, I almost always need to stop for a burger or something. Then a few hours later, I'm starving again! My body feels like it's growing out of control.

—James, age 14

Whether you're a 15-year-old girl or an 11-year-old guy, it's no secret that what you need to look and feel your best is plenty of exercise and a well-balanced diet.

Now, we can hear that audible groan from you, and it's not coming from your stomach. This isn't the first time you've heard the drill about diet and exercise, exercise and diet, yada yada yada. You're thinking, *I'm young, I got a lot of years ahead of me to eat granola and become good buddies with the Stairmaster. Why should I worry so much about my body?*

If you really think it through, you'll realize that you have a choice. If you really want to learn to be independent, to be in control, then choose to take charge of your body simply by taking good care of it.

Give this chapter a chance. Staying healthy doesn't mean you have to eat things that taste like cardboard (and besides, have you ever actually *eaten* cardboard?). It's a lot easier than you may think—and a lot more fun.

We'll give you information on what to eat and how much, how to read labels, and how to use the Food Guide Pyramid (the least known of the Great Pyramids of Egypt—kidding!), and we'll provide answers to many of your questions about food.

In the next chapter, you'll find out what exercise can and can't do for you, which exercises are dangerous, and how to plan—and stick to—a workout, exercise, or activity program.

Fuel-ups: A Guide to Eating Smart

Food is what fuels your body. You need it to live, to grow, to be active, and to feel great. Because your body is growing at a rapid rate, it needs more nutrients than it will ever need again (except during a pregnancy or if you were to nurse a baby).

All foods aren't alike. Some are high in protein, others are high in fat or carbohydrates. Your body needs a balance of all three substances to function properly.

There's a lot you should know about what you put into your mouth. Kathleen Bell, R.D., is a registered dietitian who works with kids in the Nutrition Counseling Clinic at the University of California, San Francisco. Every day she addresses questions about food from people your age. Below are her most frequently asked questions. We've provided answers in the text that follows.

❀ I just don't feel like eating when I get up in the morning. Do I really need to eat breakfast?

❀ Do athletes need a different diet than other teens?

❀ How do I know I'm meeting my nutritional needs?

❀ Who needs to take vitamin and mineral supplements?

❀ I'm trying to build muscle for the sport I'm in. Do I need extra protein?

❀ How much fluid or water should I drink in a day?

- What is the best way to lose weight?

- I'm really skinny and need to gain weight. What should I do?

- My friends and I go to fast-food places all the time. What can I eat there that's healthy?

- Is snacking between meals healthy?

- How much fiber do I need each day, and what foods are the best sources?

- I don't like milk. What else can I eat or drink to make sure I'm getting what my body needs?

- I'm a vegetarian. If I skip meat and eggs, can I still be healthy?

GOT BREAKFAST?

Breakfast is considered the most important meal of the day, yet it's the meal that is skipped the most often. *Breakfast* means "breaking the fast." While you're sleeping (8 to 12 hours), you're not eating, which means you're fasting. When you wake up, you need to jump-start your body with fuel, or break your fast. Studies show you can concentrate much better in school if you've eaten a nutritious breakfast.

If you skip breakfast because you don't have time to eat or you're trying to lose weight or you just plain don't feel hungry, you're not doing your body a favor. You're going to continue feeling sluggish until after lunch, when you've finally fueled up your body. Also, skipping breakfast means you'll probably be overly hungry by your next meal and may overeat, which isn't good for your body either.

You don't need to eat a large breakfast, but you should eat something. Here are a few great-tasting suggestions:

Quick Starts

In a blender or food processor, blend ½ cup fruited low-fat or nonfat yogurt, 1 banana, 2 tablespoons wheat germ, and a few ice cubes to create a luscious smoothie.

Top a whole-wheat toasted bagel with 1 ounce part-skim ricotta cheese and a few slices of your favorite fruit.

Combine apple slices with 1½ ounces low-fat cheese.

Cut up 1 ripe peach or 3 ripe apricots and swirl into 8 ounces low-fat or nonfat cottage cheese.

Snazz up 1 cup cooked instant oatmeal with ¼ cup applesauce and ½ teaspoon cinnamon.

High-fiber cereal (such as bran flakes) with low-fat or nonfat milk will taste better with banana slices, raisins, or whatever your favorite fruit is.

Crown a toasted whole-wheat English muffin with jam and wash it down with low-fat or nonfat milk.

Make a quickie breakfast of 3 to 6 whole-wheat or rye crackers, 1½ ounces low-fat cheese, and 1 sliced apple.

Top a toasted whole-grain waffle with fruited low-fat or nonfat yogurt and some berries.

CALORIES COUNT

If you're really active—say you work out or exercise, or engage in some strenuous activity four or more times a week—you need to consume more calories than the average teen because you burn a lot of calories while exercising. If you're an athlete, however, you do not need to load up on any one type of food.

To get those extra calories, follow the recommendations in the Food Guide Pyramid on page 99 when planning out your diet. You will *not* get fat if you consume the right amount *and* kind of calories *and* if you exercise sensibly and regularly.

The Pyramid is divided into six segments. Each features a food group. Foods in one group can't be substituted for those in another, and no one group is more important than another. A healthy diet includes foods from all of these groups. At the top of the Pyramid is Fats, Oils, and Sweets. Think of this group as "treats":

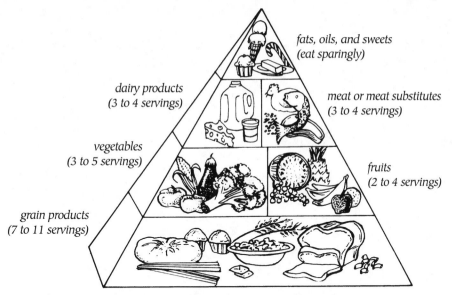

fats, oils, and sweets
(eat sparingly)

dairy products
(3 to 4 servings)

meat or meat substitutes
(3 to 4 servings)

vegetables
(3 to 5 servings)

fruits
(2 to 4 servings)

grain products
(7 to 11 servings)

Food Guide Pyramid

cookies, chips, candy, fried stuff. Eat only an occasional selection from this group—and *occasional* does not mean once a day.

The Pyramid shows how many servings of each group the average adult should eat each day. Now look at the chart "How Much Should I Eat?" on page 110. It tells you the serving size for each category, and also how many servings the average teen needs each day.

Learning what a serving size is takes a little practice. Try this: Pour yourself a bowl of cereal. Then take a measuring cup and put the poured cereal into it. You might be surprised to learn that

BEST ADVICE

Start a food diary. For one week, list everything you eat—breakfast, lunch, dinner, snacks—and how much each portion was. Make sure you include all fluids, too. At the end of the week, compare what you ate with the recommended servings on the Food Guide Pyramid. A food diary is also useful if you're trying to find out the source of a food allergy you think you may have.

what you think of as a "cup" is really 2 or even 3 cups. It's a good idea to measure your servings for a while until you become used to recognizing how much is a cup, a half cup, and so on.

VITAMINS, MINERALS, AND PROTEIN

You may need vitamin and mineral supplements if you do any of the following: diet often, have irregular eating habits, skip meals, follow a strict vegetarian diet (no meat, eggs, or dairy products), or don't eat a wide variety of foods. A multi-vitamin supplement may be enough, but check with your doctor first. Remember, though, that nutrients are better absorbed from eating the foods that contain them than from taking a supplement. For example, much of the calcium in that pill you're taking will be peed out of your body. The best thing to do is to improve your diet instead of taking a supplement.

Teens who lift weights or perform in sports that require them to build muscle think they need to eat large amounts of protein, which builds muscle and repairs tissue. This isn't true. If you're eating meats and meat alternatives such as eggs, poultry, and dairy products on a daily basis, you're most likely getting enough protein. Consuming too much protein can overwork your kidneys and cause your bones to lose calcium. Eating a wide variety of foods is the ticket.

WATER, WATER, EVERYWHERE

About 55 to 60 percent of your body weight is made up of water. Water makes your body's chemical reactions possible; lubricates your joints; washes wastes and toxins out of your body; breaks down minerals, vitamins, amino

TALK ABOUT A BUILDUP!

Several cases are on record of fecal material being stored in the bowels for more than a year. None of these people was poisoned—but they did have to deal with the discomfort of carrying around an extra 60 to 100 pounds of weight!

acids, and glucose so your body can use them; helps maintain your body temperature; and helps prevent constipation.

You've heard the oft-repeated advice about drinking eight glasses of water a day. Reports are now saying you don't have to force yourself to drink exactly this number, as long as you are drinking 6 to 8 cups of water daily.

Juices may be an OK substitute if water isn't available, but they contain a considerable amount of sugar. Milk contains protein and may stress your kidneys too much if you're already on a high-protein diet. Avoid soft drinks, because they contain more sugar than you need and really don't quench your thirst anyway.

> **BEST ADVICE**
>
> Increase your fluid intake by carrying a bottle of water with you every day and drinking from it often. Also, include clear soups or Popsicles in your diet, and take a drink every time you pass a water fountain.

Because caffeine causes your body to lose water, you will need to drink extra fluids if you drink coffee, tea, colas, and cocoa, or if you are taking cold medications, which also "dry out" your body. Better yet, cut out caffeine from your diet altogether. If you exercise regularly, you'll need even more fluids—say, 10 to 16 cups a day—depending on the intensity and duration of your activity and the air temperature in which you work out.

THE WEIGHTING GAME

Whenever people want to lose weight, their first thought usually is to cut way back on their eating—or, unfortunately, stop eating altogether. If you want to lose weight, first ask yourself whether you really need to do so. You may be feeling pressured to diet simply because you aren't as thin as that model you see in a magazine or that actor you see on TV.

As a teen, your body is growing and developing, and as a result both your height and weight are naturally increasing. *This is normal.* Think about how you are perceiving your own body. The operative word here is *perceiving*. Why are you feeling this way? How do others see you? You may want to share your thoughts with your mom or dad or a close friend and get their take on things.

If you really feel you are overweight, consult a doctor about going on a medically supervised diet.

It Doesn't Take an Einstein

Your body weight is affected by the amount of calories you take in, the amount of calories you burn during activities and exercise, and the amount of calories your body uses to function and grow.

The equation is simple: If you eat more calories than you use, you will gain weight. If you burn off more calories than you take in, you will lose weight. The key, though, is to use this equation in a healthy, smart way. Again, get your doctor's OK before you engage in any form of weight control.

Here are some smart eating tips.

❖ Eat at least three meals a day. Skipping meals will make you more hungry when you do eat, and more likely to overeat.

❖ Substitute low-fat and nonfat foods for those containing higher amounts of fat. For instance, switch to nonfat yogurt and ice cream instead of their high-fat cousins. Or, snack on a Popsicle instead of a doughnut. Remember, *fat contains twice the calories of protein and carbohydrate.* Repeat after us…

❖ Watch the salad dressing! This is one area otherwise savvy dieters overlook. Salad dressings contain a lot of fat. Use it very sparingly, or better yet, substitute the nonfat variety. At restaurants, ask for the dressing on the side so you can put on what you want.

✿ Limit the candy and sugared beverages, such as sodas and Kool-Aid. Watch for fruit juices that contain more sugar (in the form of corn syrup) than juice.

✿ Increase your activity level. Get some sort of physical exercise every day—at least 20 minutes of it—to help burn off calories. Take a short jog, go in-line skating, walk your dog, ride your bike, whatever is fun for you.

ADDING POUNDS THE HEALTHY WAY

If your goal is to put on pounds, you'll need to eat more calories than your body uses. Again, see a doctor before undertaking this.

BEST ADVICE

Don't be duped into going on one of those fad diets that tell you to eat just grapes and milk or something ridiculous like that. Three words: They don't work. A variety of foods is what's important. Try reducing your portion sizes; eat a couple bites or small scoops of ice cream instead of downing the entire pint.

Try adding two or three substantial snacks to your three square meals a day. Spreading out your meals in this manner will help you avoid that uncomfortable "stuffed" feeling. Rich desserts and fried foods are packed with calories, but they are not healthy choices, as we all know. (But they taste so *good*.) Instead, add cheese, avocado slices, and low-fat or nonfat dressing to spice up that sandwich, and try eating extra servings of grain products such as breads, pastas, and rice, as well as vegetables, fruits, and low-fat dairy products.

Super Snacking

For most teens, snacking is a way of life and a great means of refueling. You can make snack time healthy by making wise food selections. Put the following on your list:

❀ Fresh fruits and veggies.

❀ Frozen grapes, banana chunks, and berries.

❀ Snack-size boxes of raisins.

❀ Pretzels.

❀ Low-fat yogurt and cottage cheese.

❀ Smoothies (see page 97).

❀ Graham crackers, animal crackers, plain crackers.

❀ Bagels.

❀ Gingersnaps, Fig Newtons, reduced-fat cookies (this does not mean, of course, that you can eat *twice* as many of these!).

Facts About Fiber

You won't find a shred of fiber in meat or dairy products, because fiber is found only in plant foods: fruits, vegetables, grains, and legumes such as dried beans and peas.

Scientists now know that fiber-rich foods are important to your health. Fiber can't be digested. One of its functions is to act as a sponge, holding water and adding bulk to your stools, which keeps you from becoming constipated. A high-fiber, low-fat diet helps reduce your risk of diabetes, heart disease, and certain types of cancer. Fiber also can play a role in weight control, since high-fiber foods usually are quite filling. One good source of fiber is bran, which is the outer layer of grains such as wheat, oats, brown rice, and corn.

An easy way to make sure you're getting the fiber you need—20 to 35 grams a day—is to eat the suggested number of servings of vegetables, fruits, and grains in the Food Guide Pyramid. Most Americans don't consume enough fiber. If you want to increase your fiber intake, do it gradually, and be sure to drink plenty of fluids each day.

Try these fab fiber sources:

✿ Whole-wheat and whole-grain breads and crackers.

✿ Cereals containing bran as a major ingredient (OK, bran doesn't taste all that great, but if you throw a bunch of sweet fruit or yogurt on top, it actually goes down pretty well).

✿ Fresh fruits eaten with skins on.

✿ Dried fruits.

✿ Raw veggies.

✿ Legumes (cooked dried beans and peas).

✿ Nuts and seeds.

✿ Popcorn (popped in a hot-air popper, not in oil).

DEM BONES

It's only partly true that every body needs milk. What every body really needs is the mineral called calcium. Calcium not only helps build strong bones, but it also is essential to keep your heart beating, your muscles contracting, and your blood clotting. If you don't take in enough, your body will swipe it from your bones.

Until you are 24 years old, you'll need to get 1,200 milligrams of calcium a day. But you'll never outgrow your need for this mineral. Adequate supplies of calcium, plus regular exercise, will help prevent a condition called *osteoporosis* later in life. People who suffer from osteoporosis—which particularly afflicts older women—have brittle bones that break easily. Their bone density, or thickness, has decreased or thinned out.

Don't worry about counting all 1,200 of those milligrams. If you eat four servings of calcium-rich foods each day, you'll get the calcium you need. The lists on pages

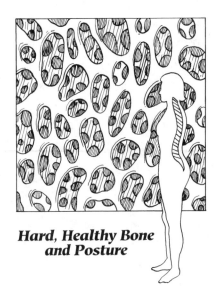

Hard, Healthy Bone and Posture

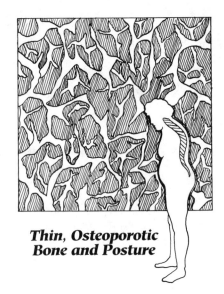

Thin, Osteoporotic Bone and Posture

106–107 will help you identify these foods and how much is considered a serving. One cup of milk, for example, is a serving. Four cups of milk a day gives you enough calcium.

Studies have shown that many teen girls do not get enough calcium because some of the foods that contain the mineral—cheese and milk, for instance—also can be high in fat and undesirable for weight-conscious teens. This may be one reason why many older adult women suffer from osteoporosis. But aside from the ready availability of nonfat milk and cheese, there are many other calcium-rich foods to choose from. Some brands of orange juice now come fortified with calcium and may contain as much as milk does.

1 serving equals:

1 cup milk or yogurt (nonfat or low-fat)

1½ ounces low-fat cheese

1 cup calcium-fortified orange juice

3 ounces canned sardines (with bones)

BONE ALONE

Only one bone in the human body does not connect to other bones: the hyoid bone, located in the throat. It supports the tongue and its muscles.

½ *serving equals:*

1 ounce calcium-fortified cereal

1 cup broccoli, kale, spinach, or greens (cooked)

3 ounces canned salmon (with bones)

4 ounces calcium-fortified tofu

¼ *serving equals:*

½ cup ice cream or frozen yogurt

½ cup cottage cheese

1 cup dried beans (cooked)

THE VEGETARIAN WAY

A lot of teens are curious about the vegetarian eating style. Some vegetarians choose to eat no meat or animal products because they love animals; in other words, they don't want to eat anything that had a  mother. Others eat a vegetarian diet because they consider it healthier.

There are several types of vegetarian diets. Lacto-ovo vegetarians eat dairy products (lacto) and eggs (ovo), but not meat, poultry, and fish. Ovo vegetarians, as you can figure out, will eat eggs as part of their diet. A vegan consumes no animal products. Those who do not eat red meat but do eat poultry and fish are not true vegetarians.

Whenever you eliminate one group of foods, you are more at risk for not getting all the nutrients you need. Except for vegans, most vegetarians get ample supplies of protein from eggs and dairy products.

Vegans must get their protein from vegetable sources and must eat a combination of what are called complementary proteins in order to get a complete protein like that found in meat and dairy. These combinations can be made up of grains and legumes (peanuts; peas; lentils; lima beans, kidney beans, soybeans, and other beans); grains and seeds; grains and nuts or nut butters; beans and seeds; nuts and seeds; or any of these combined with wheat germ or sprouts. Complementary proteins don't have to be consumed at the same meal; they can be distributed throughout the three meals eaten each day.

Here's a list of necessary nutrients and where a vegetarian can get them.

Nutrient	Source
Protein	Beans with rice; pasta with cheese; tortillas with beans; burgers and fish sticks made from soybeans; nut-butter sandwiches
Calcium	Dark green, leafy vegetables; broccoli; calcium-fortified soy products and tofu
Vitamin D	Sunshine, fortified foods, supplements
Vitamin B_{12}	Fortified soy products, supplements
Iron	Green, leafy vegetables; cooked dried beans and peas; dried fruits; food cooked in cast-iron pans
Zinc	Cooked dried beans and peas, wheat germ, whole-grain breads and cereals

SNOOPING OUT THE FAT

Fat can be sneaky. It's hidden in snacks and foods where you least expect it. We all know candy bars are synonymous with fat, but did you know microwave popcorn often is loaded with the stuff, too? Packaged cookies, cupcakes, and pastries usually contain lots of fat unless they are specifically marked "reduced fat."

We know fat lurks in salad dressings, cheese, cream cheese, doughnuts, and chips (unless they're baked instead of fried), but it also resides plentifully in creamed soups, mayonnaise, hot dogs, and sausages. And you already know to steer clear of deep-fried foods and those stir-fried in oil.

Some foods can have their fat content lowered without losing their flavor or health benefits. Whole milk, for example, contains four times as much fat as 1 percent milk and twice the fat as 2 percent milk. A smart choice is to drink low-fat or nonfat.

We've painted fat as the enemy, but don't try to eliminate all of it from your diet. Small amounts of fat are necessary for your health because fat gives you energy and helps store vitamins A, D, and E, which are needed for healthy skin and optimal body growth.

To ferret out the fat in packaged foods, learn to read labels—and then try to select foods that get 30 percent or less of their calories from fat.

Read the Label, Mabel!

To eat healthfully, you have to know what you're eating. In all that small print on the back or sides of every packaged, canned, or bottled food you pick up, you'll find lots of information.

Before you chow down on that cookie or hot dog, check out the ingredients. They're listed in descending order according to how much of each ingredient the product contains. If sugar is listed first, followed by wheat flour, sugar is the primary ingredient. Sucrose and corn syrup are forms of sugar—keep this in mind when analyzing ingredients.

Food labels are required by law to contain a section called Nutrition Facts. This tells you how many servings the package contains, how many calories are in each serving, how large the serving is, and other useful information. Some key phrases and their definitions are listed below.

❀ Light or Lite: either ⅓ fewer calories or ½ the fat per serving of the "regular" variety of that food.

❀ Sugar-free: less than ½ gram sugar per serving.

❀ Calorie-free: less than 5 calories per serving.

- ✿ Low-calorie: 40 calories or less per serving.

- ✿ Reduced-calorie: at least 25 percent less calories per serving than the regular variety.

- ✿ Fat-free: less than ½ gram fat per serving.

- ✿ Low-fat: 3 grams or less fat per serving.

- ✿ Cholesterol-free: less than 2 milligrams cholesterol and 2 grams or less saturated fat.

- ✿ Sodium-free: less than 5 milligrams sodium per serving.

Don't be fooled: Just because a product says it's "fat-free" does not mean it has absolutely no fat in it.

How Much Should I Eat?

Following are *general* guidelines for a teen girl and a teen boy.

Food Group	Servings/Day (Teen Girl)	Servings/Day (Teen Boy)	Serving Size
Dairy	2 to 4	2 to 4	I cup milk, I to 2 ounces cheese, I cup cottage cheese, I cup yogurt, I cup ice cream (all low-fat or nonfat)
Meat and Meat Substitutes	2	3	2 to 3 ounces lean meat, poultry, or fish; 2 eggs; 7 ounces tofu; 4 tablespoons peanut butter; I cup cooked legumes
Vegetables	4	5	Any type: ½ cup cooked, ½ cup chopped raw, I cup leafy green, ½ to ¾ cup juice
Fruits	3	4	I piece whole fruit or I slice melon, ¾ cup juice, ½ cup canned, ¼ cup dried
Breads, Rice, Cereals, Pasta	9	11	I slice bread, ½ cup cooked rice, or pasta, ½ cup cooked cereal, I ounce ready-to-eat cereal

THE EAT SMART FAST-FOOD MENU GUIDE

Used to be it was almost impossible to eat in a fast-food restaurant without consuming tons of fat and grease. That was before nutritionists took a good look at what was on the menu and figured out how you could eat out and still eat healthy.

Here are samples of smart choices you can make the next time you and your friends have a hankering for "fat" food. Calories are listed in parentheses.

Instead of this...	*Try this!*
Burger King	
Whopper with cheese (740)	Whopper Jr. without cheese (370)
Chocolate shake (340)	Diet soda (1)
Regular fries (210)	Green salad (60)
Total calories: 1,290	Total calories: 431
McDonald's	
Chicken McNuggets (288)	Chicken Salad Oriental (141)
Sauce (60)	Low-cal dressing (60)
12-ounce Coke (144)	12-ounce Diet Coke (1)
Total calories: 492	Total calories: 202
Taco Bell	
Burrito Supreme (457)	Taco (162)
8-ounce whole milk (150)	8-ounce nonfat milk (80)
Total calories: 607	Total calories: 242
Jack in the Box	
Ham and Swiss Burger (754)	Club Pita (277)
Onion rings (382)	Side salad (51)
	Low-cal dressing (80)
Total calories: 1,136	Total calories: 408

Wendy's

Classic Double Hamburger (680)

Small Frosty (400)

Total calories: 1,080

Single Hamburger (350)

6-ounce hot chocolate (123)

Total calories: 473

Keep these fast-food tricks in mind:

Say yes to

✿ Meat or poultry that's baked or broiled.

✿ Fresh salads and vegetables with reduced-calorie or nonfat dressings.

✿ Low-fat or nonfat milk and fruit juices.

✿ Whole-grain breads and rolls.

Say no to

✿ Any deep-fried food.

✿ Anything called "double," "jumbo," or "super."

✿ Added fats such mayonnaise, special sauces, or toppings.

✿ Desserts such as pies, cookies, and shakes.

BEST ADVICE

Ask for a nutritional brochure the next time you visit a fast-food restaurant. It will list a breakdown of all the items on the menu so you'll know how many calories and how much fat you'd be getting. You'll think twice before scarfing down that Big Mac.

CHAPTER 8

Work Out!

> I never really loved gym class, but now I kind of like it. I started to work out with the guy who lives next door, and now I feel better about my body—and myself.
>
> —Eric, age 13

You may think that exercising a lot will tire you out so much you won't be able to think straight. If you get your body moving on a regular basis—say bicycling, in-line skating, or even jump-roping every day—you'll be surprised to know that you actually will have *more* energy, think *more* clearly, and sleep *better* at night. Not only will you feel better and have more fun than your couch-potato friends, but you'll also be healthier.

Bodies in Motion

Exercise keeps both your body and your mind healthy. Without regular exercise, you won't look or feel as good as you can.

A body in motion means a happy heart, too. Your heart is the hardest-working muscle in your body—and the strongest. Whether you're asleep or awake, your heart keeps on beating, pumping blood throughout your body. With exercise, your heart can become even stronger.

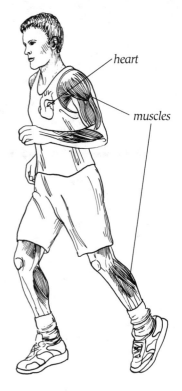

heart

muscles

Exercise also builds other muscles. That means you'll be able to do more than just ordinary things such as walking and carrying your backpack. Strong muscles will give you the power to run a mile or go rock climbing or cycle for an afternoon in the forest.

Worried about your weight? Exercise helps you maintain a healthy weight that's right for you by using up excess calories that you may take in.

You probably are pretty flexible—most teens are. You might be able to bend and jump without much trouble right now, but as you get older, you'll find that you won't move as fast as you used to—unless you keep exercising now.

Exercise also plain makes you feel good. Try exercising the next time you have a case of the blahs. The movement triggers the release of chemicals in your body called beta-endorphins, which make your brain downright giddy.

To find the most frequently asked questions that teens like you want answered, we went to fitness expert Charlie Kuntzleman, Ed.D. He's an associate professor at the University of Michigan and director of the Blue Cross/Blue Shield Fitness for Youth Program in Michigan.

❀ What is aerobic exercise, and what sports can I do to get it?

❀ I can't even bend over and touch my toes! Is something wrong with me?

❀ My grandmother says she exercises so her bones will stay healthy. I never thought bones needed exercise. What should I do to keep mine strong?

❀ I love football. If I play as often as I can, will I have a chance of making the football team at my high school?

- I'm a girl, and my friends tell me I'll get big, bulky muscles if I exercise too much. I don't want huge calves. Are they right?

- Swimming is my thing. But I've heard I should do more than just swim if I want to be fit. What else can I do?

- My butt is too big! I've seen machines on TV that are supposed to make your butt smaller. And I've heard spot reducing works, too. Do these really work?

- I'm 12 years old and skinny. If I lift lots of weights, will I look like Arnold someday?

- I'm such a klutz. I trip over things and bump into things a lot. Can I ever learn to play a sport?

- Sometimes I see athletes taking their pulse. Why are they doing this?

- Is it safe for teens to work out with weights?

A Is for Aerobic

The word *aerobic* is a fancy way of saying "needing oxygen." Aerobic exercise is any kind of activity that makes your muscles use oxygen. It's also repetitive, meaning you do it over and over again.

Running is an aerobic exercise, because you are putting one foot in front of the other repeatedly. In the meantime, your bloodstream is carrying fresh

THIRD TIME'S THE CHARM

In order to truly benefit from any aerobic activity, you must do it at least three times a week for 20 to 30 minutes without stopping. One reason for this is to increase your heart rate to a level that is beneficial.

oxygen to your muscles, including your heart. Fast walking, dancing, rowing, in-line skating, swimming, cross-country skiing, bicycling, jumping rope, and playing basketball, soccer, or hockey are all aerobic activities.

Toe the Line

If you can't bend over and touch your toes—be glad. And if you can, stop doing it. Exercise physiologists—the experts who study the proper way to exercise—have discovered that toe touching is a surefire way to injure your back. Another exercise to avoid is a straight-leg sit-up. Sit-ups are great for working your abdominal muscles—your abs—but they should be done with your knees bent to avoid injury.

Engage in these activities to increase your flexibility instead: gymnastics, ballet, yoga, or any of the martial arts such as tae kwon do and karate.

Be Good to Your Bones

Certain types of weight-bearing exercise are as important as eating calcium-rich foods for strengthening your bones. Aerobic dance, baseball, basketball, tennis, soccer, weight lifting, running, dancing, and brisk walking are all weight-bearing activities. These exercises stress your bones—*good* stress, mind you—which makes them denser and therefore stronger.

To make sure all your bones get a workout, you should include a variety of activities in your workout program. This is called *cross-training*. Running, for instance, will strengthen the bones in your legs, but not those in your arms. Lifting light weights or doing gymnastics will work those arm bones.

If you don't do exercise that puts stress on your bones, you may become a candidate for osteoporosis when you are older. People don't realize they have osteoporosis until they suddenly break a hip, a wrist, a leg, or an arm. The bones have become so fragile over time that they break easily. In the United States, this crippling disease affects more than 25 million women and 5 million men.

Train Like a Pro

Is there a particular sport you just love to play? The best way to get your body in shape for that sport is to do more than just play that sport.

Professional athletes do this all the time. Besides their own game, they also do aerobic exercises or run to build up their stamina and make their heart work more efficiently. Some even take ballet lessons to improve their timing. Most pros train with weights, not only to build muscles but also to strengthen bones. To relax on their days off, a lot of pros play golf, which is believed to be beneficial for one's mental health.

Try doing a variety of activities—it'll help you improve your game, whether it's figure skating, wrestling, baseball, or football.

The Muscle Mind-Set

Misinformed people—both guys and girls—tell girls that exercise builds up "ugly" muscles. They are wrong, wrong, wrong. Exercise is as good for girls as it is for guys. There is no exercise and no sport that isn't great for both sexes.

Exercise—even weight lifting—will not result in bulky bodybuilder-type muscles on girls. It will increase muscle strength and skin tone, but if you're a girl, it won't make you look like a female Schwarzenegger. In general, girls cannot build muscles like guys because their bodies are not genetically designed to become as heavily muscled as guys' bodies are.

Water Babies

Swimming laps is a fabulously beneficial physical activity. It doesn't stress your joints, it's aerobic (working your heart and lungs), and it builds muscle—just look at the shoulders of Olympic swimmers.

What swimming doesn't do, though, is help strengthen your bones. Even if you hit the pool seven days a week, you'll still have to do weight-bearing activities along with your swim routine. Play a sport regularly or do some running or brisk walking to help build those bones. Check out the chart on pages 126–27 to help you decide which activity you'd like to try.

Tighten That Tush

Lots of teens—and adults, too—think that one or more parts of their bodies are too big, too little, or just not great-looking. Television infomercials advertise all kinds of gadgets and gizmos that promise to reduce your butt while you just lie there.

If you were to buy one of these machines, all you would lose is your money. They don't work, and neither does spot reducing. You can lower your body fat through vigorous exercise and reducing the amount of calories you eat, but there is no guarantee that you will lose fat from any one place on your body. The size of your bottom, or your hips, or your thighs, or even your arms depends on your body type, and your body type is what you've inherited from your parents.

You can, however, firm up your butt through exercise. Try bike riding, stair stepping, or any sport on the chart on pages 126–27 that works your lower body.

But Why Can't I Look Like Arnold or Cindy?

If you take a good look around, you'll see that people come in all shapes and sizes. You might adore Arnold's pecs, but unless you have his particular body type, you won't develop muscles like his even if you lifted weights 24 hours a day—which is downright dangerous, we might add. Kids, don't try this at home.

There are three general body types. The mesomorph—Arnold's type—has low-to-medium body fat, large bones, and large muscles. The ectomorph has low body fat, very small bones, and small muscles. Cindy Crawford and many of those tall, slim models fall into this category—a very small number in comparison with the global population. The endomorph is characterized by a high percentage of body fat, large bones, and small muscles.

Most people are actually a *combination* of two or three types. Although you can't change the type of body you were born with, you can look and feel great about your body by developing healthy eating habits and exercising regularly.

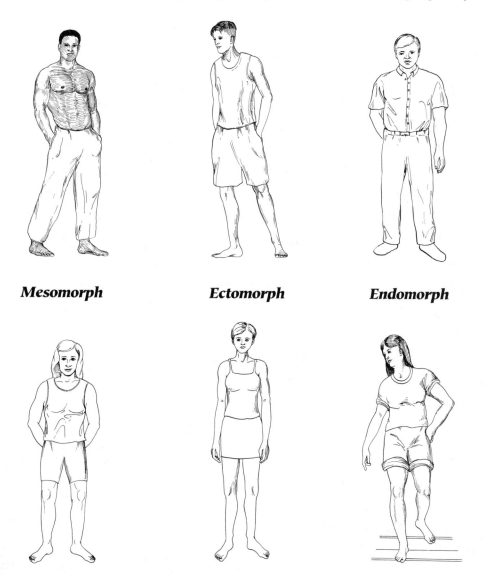

Mesomorph   **Ectomorph**   **Endomorph**

The Complete Klutz

Even superathletes felt clumsy and awkward when they were starting out. It's a sure bet that figure-skating champions Tara Lipinski and Michelle Kwan fell down *a lot* before they went on to win their Olympic medals. Basketball greats Magic Johnson and Michael Jordan tripped over their feet a time or two—or more—before going on to become two of the best hoopsters in the world.

No one starts out a champ, but by playing sports or running or working out, you'll train your body to move more gracefully. And you'll have a lot of fun, too.

Heart Watch

While running, jogging, or even swimming, some people wear watches to monitor their heart rate. After taking their pulse, they use a simple formula to figure out how many times their heart is beating per minute.

Your heart deserves a good workout on a regular basis—but it also must be a safe workout. You can monitor how hard your heart is working during aerobic exercise by learning to take your pulse and then finding your Target Heart Rate Range. This range has a low number and a high number. Your goal is to get your heart rate somewhere between these numbers while exercising.

Taking Your Pulse

Place your index and middle fingers on the radial artery on the underside of your wrist, about 1 to 2 inches below the base of your thumb. Then, count the "beats"

TICK... TICK... TICK

If we assume that the heart beats at least once every second, then the heart of a person who is 70 years old will have gone through at least 2.8 billion beats.

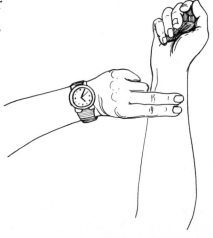

that you feel. Look at the second hand on a watch or a nearby clock. Count the beats for 15 seconds. Multiply that number by 4 to get your heart rate, or the number of pulses per minute.

Finding Your Target Heart Rate Range

During your workout, your heart rate should stay within a safe but beneficial range for your age. This is called the Target Heart Rate Range. The formula is very easy to memorize and use, and looks a lot more complicated than it really is. As a sample, here's how a 15-year-old teen would do the calculations:

Start with this number:	220
Subtract your age:	–15
	———
	205

205 is this teen's maximum heart rate. Now, multiply by .60:

$$205 \times .60 = 123$$

and by .80:

$$205 \times .80 = 164$$

The Target Heart Rate Range for this teen is between 123 and 164 beats. Now, determine your own range. The next time you're doing an aerobic workout, take your pulse and see if it falls within your Target Heart Rate Range. If it doesn't, you're probably not exercising long enough or hard enough. And remember, before you launch any vigorous exercise program, get your doctor's approval.

Pumping Iron

It wasn't long ago that experts believed young people shouldn't work out with weights. Those times have changed. Now doctors say it's OK for teens to lift weights.

But there's a catch: NEVER, ever lift weights by yourself or with someone who isn't skilled at weight lifting. Your best bet is to work out at a gym where you can team up with a trainer. Even professional weight lifters use a spotter, a trained person who stands next to the lifter to catch the weight if the lifter loses control.

Building an Exercise Program

To create your own effective workout program, it's important to know what makes good, sensible exercise.

Stretching and warming up before engaging in any exercise is necessary if you want to avoid injury. Many people skip this step, which is risky. Warming up helps protect your muscles and bones from damage during the more vigorous exercise. It can help relax and clear your mind, too. Before you exercise, do 10 minutes of stretching and warming up.

We've included some warm-up exercises below.

Cross-Overs

Standing straight, extend your left arm out to the side, palm up. Bend at the waist in the same direction, bringing your right arm over your head until your right palm meets your left palm. Do this 10 times. Repeat using your right arm and bending to the right, also 10 times.

Punch the Sky

Standing straight, look up and extend your right arm straight up, making a fist and tilting your body slightly toward the right. Lower your arm. Repeat with your left arm. Do this 10 times, alternating arms.

Do the Twist

While standing, bend your elbows and place your hands on your waist. Twist your body gently at the waist side to side 10 times.

The Butterfly

Sit down and bend your legs to bring the soles of your feet together. Using your elbows, gently press your knees toward the floor. Hold for 10 counts. Now slowly press your chest toward your feet. Hold for another 10 counts. Repeat this entire exercise 10 times.

The Dolphin-Kitty

Lie on your stomach and lift your head up. Place your hands in front of you and gently push your upper body up, stretching your lower back. Bring your body up so that you are on your hands and knees. Arch your back, keeping your head and shoulder toward the floor. Repeat 10 times.

The Straddle

Sit on the floor and spread your legs wide. Reach both arms toward your right foot and hold for 10 counts. Reach both arms toward your left foot and hold for another 10. Reach both arms toward the center and hold for 10. Repeat this exercise 5 times.

MAKING EXERCISE A PART OF YOUR LIFE: A GAME PLAN

It's time to get physical! To put together your own program, we've provided tips on what kinds of exercises to do when you're alone, when you're with a buddy, and when you've rounded up a bunch of your fellow fitness freaks. Experiment to see which ones suit you, and come up with your own ideas as well.

Alone Again (Naturally)

When it's just me, myself, and I, try the following:

✿ Pop an exercise video into the VCR. Your local video store has lots of cassettes for rent. Check out a few and find one to your liking. If aerobics are not your thing, try videos on weight training, jazz dance, or martial arts. If it's new to you, who knows—you might love it!

✿ Get out your bicycle, grab your helmet, and go for a ride. Be sure to tell your mom, dad, or older sibling the route you'll be taking.

✿ Take Fido for a walk or, better yet, a run or jog. Dogs need exercise as much as you do. If your pooch is old, overweight, or just plain out of shape, start out with a nice walk. Dogs also need to develop their fitness levels slowly, just like people do.

✿ If you have a large backyard, run short-distance sprints. On hot days it's fun and refreshing to run through the sprinklers.

✿ See how many jumping jacks you can do, or how long you can hop on one foot.

✿ Turn on the radio and dance. It's a snap to imitate the moves you see on MTV's *Global Groove,* but why not invent some cool moves of your own?

✿ Run up and down the stairs in your home or the stairs at a local public building.

✿ Do something nice for a neighbor: mow the lawn, take out the trash, or sweep the sidewalk. You'll get a little workout and lend a helping hand at the same time.

BEST ADVICE

The hardest part of exercising is sticking to a program. Set aside a time for your workout (around the same time each day will help establish the routine). Then make a firm commitment and follow through, and you'll soon realize how good you feel. Try recruiting a friend to exercise with, so each of you can motivate the other.

Two's Company

Team up with your best bud, your brother or sister, or that cute guy or girl you've been dying to get to know better.

❀ Indoors, hunker down over a game of Ping-Pong. Outdoors, start up a game of badminton or one-on-one volleyball. If you don't have a net, use a rope as a substitute.

❀ Is there a hoop nearby? Play some one-on-one basketball! If others want to run with you two, this activity graduates to the next section (The Gang's All Here).

❀ Have a jump-rope competition.

❀ Go for a bike ride. Look for some fairly steep hills to get a really good workout.

The Gang's All Here

Group activities offer a great combination of fun, exercise, and friendship.

❀ Organize a game of baseball, broomball, kickball, soccer, or, if everyone has skates and sticks, roller hockey. You don't have to keep score—just play for fun.

❀ If there's a safe place to ride near your house or in your neighborhood, play Follow the Leader on your bicycles. Wear your helmets!

❀ Get out a stopwatch or plain wristwatch and hold a bike race. Plot the route together and see who can cycle it in the fastest time.

❀ Tune in to your favorite radio station or put on your favorite CDs and have a dance party.

GIVE THE Y A TRY

Your local YMCA is a great place to work out. Most YMCAs offer special programs for teens. It's also a great place to become skilled at new-to-you sports and make new friends who share your interests. Unlike health clubs for adults, memberships at the Y are affordable even for teens.

THE RATE-YOUR-SPORT CHART

By now you know that to get the workout that's best for your body, you should put together a program of cross-training; that is, one that includes activities that work out all parts of your body.

Find out what certain sports or activities can do for you by using the chart below. Each is rated according to the level of effectiveness on your body. Keep in mind that you want to work your heart as well as your upper and lower body. Only a few sports give you a "total" workout, so play a variety to keep yourself in top shape.

Sport	Aerobic Workout	Upper Body Strength	Lower Body Strength	Flexibility
Aerobic dance	Good to fair	Fair	Good	Good
Backpacking	Good to fair	Fair	Good	Fair
Badminton	Good to fair	Fair	Fair	Fair
Baseball and softball	Fair to poor	Fair	Fair	Fair
Bicycling	Excellent	Fair	Excellent	Fair
Bowling	Poor	Fair	Poor	Poor
Canoeing	Good to fair	Good	Poor	Poor
Football	Good to fair	Fair	Good	Good to fair
Golf	Poor	Fair	Good	Fair
Karate	Fair	Good	Good	Excellent
Racquetball	Good	Good	Good	Fair
Running	Excellent	Poor	Good	Poor
Skating	Good to fair	Poor	Good	Fair
Skiing (cross-country)	Excellent	Good	Excellent	Good
Skiing (downhill)	Fair	Good	Good	Good

Sport	Aerobic Workout	Upper Body Strength	Lower Body Strength	Flexibility
Soccer	Excellent	Fair	Excellent	Good
Swimming	Excellent	Good	Good	Good
Tennis	Good to fair	Good	Good	Fair
Volleyball	Good	Fair	Good	Fair
Walking	Good	Poor	Good	Fair
Water skiing	Poor	Good	Good	Fair
Weight training	Poor to fair	Excellent	Excellent	Fair

Body Breakdowns

A couple of days ago I noticed one of the kids in my neighborhood and some of the kids at school were having problems. One has trouble breathing when we play sports. Another has to eat a lot, even during a volleyball game. I'd like to find out what's wrong with them, but I guess I'm too shy to ask.

—Ruthie, age 14

When you were a little kid, you probably didn't pay attention to a lot that was going on around you. Adolescence seems to be the time when you start to become aware of what's happening to your friends at school and other people you come in contact with. You're learning how to build relationships, and because of that, you're concerned about your friends' well-being.

The More You Know

If you watch the news on TV and read the newspaper, you already know bad things—diseases, accidents, even death—can happen to almost anyone. Learning the facts about a disease, a condition, or a dangerous behavior can help ease some of the worries you might have, not only about your friends and your family, but about yourself, too.

Alan Greene, M.D., is a Northern California pediatrician—a doctor who specializes in treating children and teens—and a professor at Stanford University School of Medicine. He talks to so many kids that he sometimes knows what they want to know about before they even ask! Dr. Greene has a Web site (www.drgreene.com) where you can ask him questions yourself, or read the answers to questions other kids have asked.

Here are some of the more common questions Dr. Greene gets asked. They'll be answered in the text that follows.

✿ My parents think there's something wrong with me because I like to stay up late and sleep in in the morning. On school nights I can't sleep as late as I'd like, so I get really sleepy during the day. Am I weird?

✿ I never talk about this with anyone, not even my best friend. I wet the bed. How can I make myself stop?

✿ A guy at school has to give himself a shot of something called insulin a couple of times a day. Why?

✿ My best friend has a cousin who has scoliosis. I've never heard of this disease. What is it?

✿ One of the girls in my PE class gets a lot of infections. She calls them UTI. She won't tell me what it means. Is it something contagious?

✿ What is cancer, anyway? Should a teen be scared of it?

✿ My big brother is away at college. His last letter talked about some people in his dorm getting mono. What's that?

✿ Last week I saw some kids smoking bidis. They said they are "natural" and come in flavors like chocolate, vanilla, and cherry. Are they safe?

Night Owls and Body Clocks

Did you know that your body has a built-in clock? It tells you when to go to sleep and when to get up. Researchers at the National Sleep Foundation believe that during puberty, the hormones your body is producing sometimes "reset" your body clock. This explains why you might like to stay up late and then sleep until noon.

Unfortunately, if you do stay up as late as you want, you still have to get up in time for school. This means you'll be missing the sleep that your body needs. Sleep experts say that the average teen needs about 9 hours of sleep each night, but that many teens get less than 7 hours.

If you find yourself feeling sleepy during the day, or if you fall asleep during class, or if you're especially cranky on certain days, your body clock might be in need of a readjustment. Try these solutions:

❀ Go to bed 15 minutes earlier each night, until you're going to bed at a time when you can get in 9 hours of sleep.

❀ When you wake up in the morning, start your day with a little exercise and some sunshine. This will make you feel more alert and help reset your wake/sleep body clock.

❀ Don't take naps after school even if you feel tired. Napping will only keep you awake at night.

The Bed-Wetter Blues

You don't have to feel like the Lone Stranger if you have "accidents" while you're asleep. Six million other teens your age in America share the same problem. It's nothing to be ashamed of, and it's not your fault!

The medical term to describe bed-wetting is *enuresis*. For many years researchers didn't know what caused teens—and even some adults—to wet the bed. Now they know one of the reasons.

As you know, our brain produces lots of hormones. One of these, called anti-diuretic hormone, or ADH, is responsible for allowing us to sleep through the night without urinating. Some kids don't produce enough ADH. Another reason is that some people may have a bladder that's too small to hold all the urine they produce.

If you have tried all the usual treatments—"alarms," not drinking fluids after a certain time, having your parents get you up at night, cutting out colas and other caffeinated drinks from your diet—and you still can't stay dry at night, Dr. Greene suggests trying the Potty Pager, an alarm specially designed for teens. For more information, call 1-800-497-6573 or log on to www.pottypager.com.

Another breakthrough for bed wetters is a prescription medication called DDAVP (desmopressin acetate). Until recently this medication had to be refrigerated, but no longer. Now, campers and those who love to go on overnight trips can take it along. As with all medications, ask your doctor if DDAVP will work for you.

Another great resource for information about bed-wetting is the National Kidney Foundation. Call 1-800-622-9010 and ask for a referral to a doctor in your area who is sympathetic to your problem and who can help.

The ABC's of Diabetes

Do you know a guy who never drinks soda? Do you have a friend who has to go home to check her blood sugar before she can meet you to go in-line skating? They may have diabetes, a disease that more than 100,000 American kids live with every day.

You can't catch diabetes from someone who has it. The type that affects kids is called insulin-dependent diabetes. This means that their bodies can't manufacture a hormone called insulin.

When you eat, your body takes the sugar it gets from food and turns it into a fuel called glucose. Glucose needs insulin in order to enter the cells of your body and provide it with energy. Insulin is made by the pancreas, an organ located next to your stomach. If the pancreas is not functioning properly it will not produce enough insulin. The glucose then stays in your bloodstream and eventually leaves your body through your urine.

The test doctors use to detect diabetes is simple. A special strip of paper is dipped into a urine sample. If the strip detects glucose in the urine, the person has tested positive for diabetes.

Those with diabetes have to give themselves insulin by injecting it into their bodies with a needle, usually two times a day. This injected insulin works just like the insulin that the pancreas naturally produces. First, the person tests her glucose by pricking a finger with a small needle called a lancet. The drop of blood is spread on a strip and inserted into a device that determines how much glucose her blood contains. That tells her how much insulin she needs to inject. If she does not give herself insulin, she will become fatigued and lose weight and, in the worst-case scenario, may lapse into a coma.

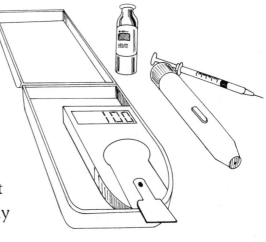

Devices for Testing Glucose

Those who keep their diabetes in check enjoy healthy, normal lifestyles, just like those who do not have the disease. If you don't see someone injecting, you may not even know that person has diabetes. Kids with diabetes aren't much different from kids without diabetes, except that they have to monitor their blood sugar regularly. Like all kids, they have to eat healthy foods and get the correct amount of exercise every day.

If you'd like to learn more about diabetes, visit www.childrenwithdiabetes.com. It has plenty of helpful information, some of it provided by kids with diabetes.

Straight Talk About Scoliosis

You couldn't walk, run, or play if your spine didn't curve a little bit. But some teens' spines curve too much—so much that they have a condition called *scoliosis*. The word *scoliosis* is from the Greek word *skoliosis,* which means "curvature."

In scoliosis, the spine gradually curves from side to side until it ends up in an S shape. A mild curve generally doesn't need to be treated, whereas a more severe curve can be uncomfortable and require treatment such as wearing a back brace or having surgery.

Scoliosis is somewhat of a mystery. Doctors don't know what causes it, but they do know how to treat it. A person might be born with it (it is hereditary), or it can develop over time. Usually it is diagnosed between ages 10 and 14, and it occurs five times as often in girls as it does in guys. The disease can be hard to diagnose because it happens so gradually, and unless it's severe it's usually painless.

If you live in a state that tests for scoliosis, you'll probably be given a forward-bending test. A nurse or a teacher will have you remove your shirt and then will ask you to bend over so that your back is parallel to the floor while he checks your spine. It's simple and painless.

If your state doesn't require such a test, your doctor probably will perform one when you have a physical examination. A teen who has scoliosis can do pretty much whatever any teen can do.

The Scoop on UTI

UTI is medical shorthand for urinary tract infection, a common infection among teens and some adults as well. The urinary tract is made up of your urethra, your bladder, and your kidneys, and the tubes that connect them. (Refer to the illustrations in chapters 2 and 3 to see where the urinary tract is located.) UTIs can cause pain and discomfort, but they can be quickly and easily treated by a doctor.

A UTI develops when a bacterium called *E. coli* enter the urethra. This bacterium is commonly found in the digestive tract and around the vagina and the rectum and usually is harmless. It's when it gets into the urethra that it causes problems. The warm, moist environment of the urethra and bladder makes the bacterium grow and multiply.

The symptoms of UTI are easy to recognize. If the infection is in the bladder (called *cystitis*) or urethra, you'll feel a burning sensation during urination. You also might have to urinate frequently, or you might feel as though you have to pee all the time, but only a little urine comes out. Pain in your lower back or in your genital area is another symptom. Blood might show up in your urine, or your urine might have a foul smell.

Girls are more prone to UTIs because their urethras are much shorter: about 2 inches compared with 8 or 9 inches in guys. The short length of the urethra makes it easier for bacteria to travel up to the bladder.

Remember, a doctor must treat this infection with antibiotics. It is important that you see one as soon as you notice these symptoms.

A kidney infection can be much more serious. It has some of the same symptoms as a UTI plus fever, chills, and sometimes nausea. Kidney infections require *immediate* medical attention. Your doctor will prescribe medicine to clear up the infection. These medications work quickly, but you must follow your doctor's instructions and take the medication for as long as she says you should.

Antibiotics are the most effective treatment for UTIs, but they won't keep them from occurring again. The best method is prevention. Practice the following:

❁ Don't "hold" your urine in; urinating frequently washes away bacteria and helps prevent infection.

❁ Drink plenty of water throughout the day so that you pee more often. Avoid caffeine, which irritates the bladder. Even decaf coffee still contains some caffeine.

❀ Drink cranberry juice. Cranberries contain a substance that helps prevent bacteria from adhering to the wall of the bladder.

❀ Girls should wipe with toilet tissue from front to back, not back to front. This keeps bacteria away from the opening of the urethra.

❀ Both girls and guys should keep their genital areas clean and dry. Girls should not use bubble-bath products—these can irritate the urethra—and should change tampons and sanitary pads often during their period (see chapter 2).

Understanding Cancer

It's known as the Big C. To both teens and adults, the word *cancer* is scary. This may be because they don't know what cancer really is, or that many types of cancer can now be treated and cured.

Our bodies are made up of millions of cells—tiny units that grow and die. Sometimes, some of these cells start to grow and grow on their own. These out-of-control cells may join together to form tumors or abnormal lumps—cancer—that spread and destroy normal cells.

Experts don't know why some people get cancer and others don't, but they do know that it is not contagious. Cancer is rarely seen in kids and teens—only 14 in 100,000 will get cancer. At your age, the odds are low that you will get it.

Several forms of treatment have emerged over the years. Radiation (invisible high-energy waves) is used to zap and destroy tumors. Cancerous tumors are removed during surgery. Chemotherapy, which consists of special drugs designed to kill cancer cells, is a common treatment. Today, more and more kids and adults who have cancer are successfully treated and go on to live happy and cancer-free lives.

Into Thin Air

Can you imagine what it would be like if you could hardly breathe? Or what it would feel like if you had to breathe through a straw?

Asthma is a condition that affects about 5 million young people, or about one out of every ten. Those with this condition have very sensitive bronchial tubes—

those that supply air to the lungs. When these tubes become irritated, they become narrow, making it difficult to breathe and bringing on what is called an *asthma attack*. Most of the time, those with asthma function just fine—it's only during an attack that they have trouble breathing.

You can't catch asthma, but you can inherit a tendency to have it from one or both of your parents. Rapid breathing, coughing, and wheezing are all symptoms of an asthma attack. The attack can be triggered by certain conditions such as exercise, an infection, allergies, or irritants such as cigarette smoke, paint fumes, household dust, and pollen from plants. Some say that the weather or breathing cold air can cause an attack.

Although asthma can't be cured, it can be controlled. Kids and teens can learn to avoid conditions that cause asthma attacks, and doctors can prescribe medications to make breathing easier.

If I Look Good, Will I Feel Good?

You may have heard someone say that his friend has an eating disorder, or you may even have a friend who is getting thinner and thinner even though she insists she is fat.

Doctors believe that as many as 7 million people in the United States have an eating disorder. Two of the most serious are *anorexia nervosa*, which means "without appetite," and *bulimia*, which means "appetite of an ox."

ANOREXIA: STARVING TO DEATH

Anorexia usually begins when a person goes on a diet and then becomes obsessed with losing weight. This person eventually becomes fearful of becoming fat. She eats almost nothing at all, and often exercises so much that whatever food she does eat is quickly burned up.

When a person with anorexia looks in a mirror, what she sees is a fat, bloated person, even though her family and friends see the opposite. It is her *perception*, not the *reality*, that has led to her anorexia. Experts do not know the exact cause

of anorexia, but they believe its victims
feel that the only thing they have
control over in life is their eating,
their weight, and the amount of
exercise they do.

Eating disorders are seen more
often in girls than in boys. However,
this is not to minimize its effect on
guys who do develop a disorder.
Many of these boys are involved in
a sport such as wrestling, in which
they are pressured to lose weight—
called "cutting weight"—in order to qualify in their category.

With girls, there is more pressure from society to look thin, and that to look
thin is to look beautiful—which, of course, is wrong. Images in magazines, on bill-
boards, and on film and TV show super-skinny models and actresses, and many
young girls see them as role models. These women sometimes are abnormally
thin—much thinner, in fact, than a normal girl can ever expect to be. It is impossible to live up to the standards seen in the media.

Anorexia is a damaging, dangerous, and life-threatening disorder. It generally begins
when a girl is in her early teens, but it has been diagnosed in girls as young as 10.

Here are some warning signs:

❀ Being preoccupied, even obsessed, with how much one weighs and the size of
   clothes one wears. The person thinks and talks about her weight and body
   size constantly.

❀ Denying that one feels hungry.

❀ Insisting that one feels fat.

❀ Spending most of one's time alone.

❀ Exercising excessively—at school, in the bathroom, in bed, and so forth.

Without treatment, anorexics may, literally, starve themselves to death. The key—and the hardest part—is to get a person to admit that she has anorexia and wants help. If someone you know is showing the above warning signs, and talking with her hasn't helped, don't keep it a secret. Talk with your mom or dad or a school counselor about your concerns for your friend. Or, call any of the hotlines listed at the back of this book.

BULIMIA: THE BINGE-AND-PURGE CYCLE

Bulimia also affects young women and adolescent girls. Unlike the person with anorexia, the person with this disorder eats a lot, stuffing herself with whatever she can get her hands on—this is called *bingeing*. Afterward, she

DYING TO BE THIN

One study showed that anorexic girls estimated their bodies to be 74 percent larger than their actual size. Many anorexics resist getting help because they are afraid of gaining weight or of being criticized. Every year, 2 to 8 percent of anorexics die.

makes herself throw up the food she ate—this is called *purging*—by sticking her finger down her throat or taking laxatives, a form of medicine that causes bowel movements. Taking laxatives can become dangerously habit-forming.

Unlike anorexia, girls with bulimia are rarely thin. They usually are of normal weight or just slightly overweight, which makes this disorder harder to detect.

The person with bulimia can suffer many bad and long-term side effects from constant vomiting. She experiences pain in her stomach and abdominal area. The acid that comes up from her stomach while vomiting can cause tooth decay. She may develop "chipmunk cheeks," which happens when the salivary glands in the mouth expand permanently from constant irritation. Girls with bulimia can even have a heart attack. Here are some warning signs of bulimia:

✿ Spending most of one's time alone.

✿ Eating a lot of food but not gaining weight.

❀ Making up excuses for going to the bathroom after eating large amounts of food.

❀ Using laxatives and diuretics (diuretics are medications or fluids—such as coffee—that cause one to urinate).

The good news is that both anorexia and bulimia can be treated, but only under the supervision of both a medical doctor and a psychotherapist. The medical doctor helps get the person back on track physically, while the therapist is needed to help the person deal with her distorted body image and learn healthy ways to maintain her weight and self-esteem.

The Facts About Mono

You may have heard about something called "the kissing disease." The medical term for it is *mononucleosis,* or "mono" for short. Anyone can get this virus, but it's most frequently seen in young people between the ages of 10 and 25.

Mononucleosis may have a cute nickname, but it's no joke. Mono can wipe you out for a week or even up to several months. It is caused by the Epstein-Barr virus, one of the herpes viruses. This virus affects blood cells and your salivary glands.

You can catch mono when you are exposed to infected saliva—drinking from an infected person's glass, using an infected person's straw, being exposed to a sneeze from an infected person, even using a telephone that's been contaminated by saliva. Of course, you can get it by kissing someone on the mouth who is already infected, but you do not even need to actually touch the person—close contact is all it takes. Once you've been exposed to the virus, it takes one to two weeks for symptoms to crop up.

Mono's main symptom is that you feel very, very tired. These are some other signs:

❀ Sore throat.

❀ Fever.

- ❀ Swollen lymph glands (small glands found under your arms, in your groin area, and in your neck).

- ❀ Sore muscles.

- ❀ Headache.

- ❀ Enlarged liver and/or spleen (organs located in your abdomen that filter out impurities from your body).

Your doctor can tell if you have mono by doing a simple blood test. If you have a fever plus one or more of the other symptoms, make an appointment.

Unfortunately, there is no magic pill that cures mono. You'll need to rest, eat plenty of nutritious foods, and drink liquids to kill the kissing disease. Your doctor will tell you what type of medication to take to reduce your fever and when you can return to school and resume your regular activities.

If you do get mono, don't spread it around. Follow these anti-contagion rules:

- ❀ Use only your own eating and drinking utensils. Don't let others use them while you're sick. If they must be used, make sure they are thoroughly sanitized in soap and hot water.

- ❀ Cover your mouth and nose if you have to cough or sneeze.

- ❀ Wipe off the mouthpiece of the telephone with rubbing alcohol when you're finished using it.

Tobacco, Alcohol, and Drugs

Bad habits or, worse yet, addictions, can sneak right up on you. Somebody offers you a cigarette, a puff off a marijuana joint, a chunk of tobacco to chew, or a sip of booze. Your mind tells you to say no, but you just might eventually accept the offer out of curiousity. After all, one wouldn't hurt, right?

This is exactly how addictive habits begin. No one, not even adults, thinks that having "just one" of anything—cigarette, drink, snort of cocaine—can lead to a lifetime of addiction.

Unfortunately, it can. When you think you won't be happy until you have another hit, or you won't be able to get through the day without another drink, or you just need to feel another cigarette in your hand, you have an addiction.

BEST ADVICE

Be smart and don't give any of the following even a try: tobacco, alcohol, or drugs of any kind!

Saying no to people who offer you tobacco, alcohol, or drugs takes guts. Don't worry about offending them. Why should you care what they think? You'll be surprised to know that most of the time they'll just drop the issue and won't ask you again. But sometimes they might call you a wimp or tell you that you're not cool. Major peer pressure! It's something we all have to deal with at some point. Keep in mind that anyone who offers you something that's dangerous obviously doesn't care about your well-being—or theirs, for that matter.

The most practical reason for not smoking, drinking, or taking drugs is that these bad habits are expensive. Why waste your money on something that can kill you when you could be spending it on movies, CDs, clothes, computer games, sports equipment, concerts, or your favorite hobby?

THE TOBACCO TRAP

Tobacco contains nicotine, a chemical that's addictive. The more nicotine you put into your body, the more your body will crave it. But nicotine isn't the only reason that tobacco is dangerous.

Cigarettes also contain thousands of other dangerous chemicals. Read the list below, then ask yourself if you really want to put any of these in your body.

✿ Formaldehyde (the liquid used to preserve dead animals).

✿ Arsenic (a poison used in insecticides and weed killers).

✿ Cadmium (a metal used to make car batteries).

✿ Lead (yes, the same stuff that kills brain cells).

✿ Cyanide (a deadly poison).

✿ Benzine (a poisonous liquid sometimes used in high-performance race cars).

In addition to filling your body with poisons and toxins, cigarette smoking is becoming increasingly inconvenient and uncool. Most airlines and more and more restaurants are banning smoking. You will most likely have to step outside every time you want to light up. You can't smoke at most indoor facilities: theaters, skating rinks, shopping malls—every place that's cool to hang out at. It's more convenient *not* to smoke, so why start?

BEWARE OF BIDIS

Bidis—"dessert-flavored" cigarettes—are the latest trend on school and college campuses. They're just another way for greedy and unscrupulous adults to make money by getting teens hooked on nicotine.

A bidi is a small, cheaply made item that is derived from Indian imports called beedies. It comes in flavors such as chocolate, vanilla, and cinnamon to appeal to kids and teens. A colorful piece of thread is tied at each end—another touch designed to make you think bidis are groovy. It is about half the diameter of a regular cigarette and looks more like a joint, which also appeals to kids.

The truth is, bidis are even MORE dangerous than cigarettes because they contain more nicotine: 8 percent compared to 1 to 2 percent in regular American cigarettes.

Bidis are not a new creation, although some people may tell you they are. They have been sold in poorer nations for hundreds of years. They are TOTALLY unsafe to smoke. Bidis cause cancer of the tongue, gums, mouth, esophagus, lungs, and voice box, as well as high blood pressure, heart disease, and stunted growth. Bidis are a death trip.

Spit It Out!

Tobacco companies won't admit it, but they need to keep recruiting new, young smokers to buy their products and to, sadly, replace the older smokers who suffer from emphysema and have died from lung cancer. If these companies can't get you to smoke cigarettes through their advertising, they don't give up there. As an alternative, they try to get you to start using chewing tobacco and snuff.

Both of these products contain nicotine. Both are very addictive. Some users say they are even harder to quit than cigarettes. Chewing tobacco is, well, just what it says. Snuff is a powdered tobacco that can be inhaled, chewed, or placed against the gums.

Here's how snuff and chewing tobacco will affect you:

- ✿ They cause your lips and gums to crack and bleed.
- ✿ They cause your gums to recede, which leads to tooth loss.
- ✿ Inhaling snuff irritates and damages the inner lining of your nose.
- ✿ They speed up your heart rate and cause irregular heartbeats, both of which lead to brain damage and heart attack.
- ✿ They may cause throat and mouth cancer.
- ✿ They color your teeth brown.
- ✿ They make you spit out lots of brown slime. Not a pretty sight.
- ✿ They make your breath stink.

ALCOHOL AND YOU

Is it hip to drink? Not really, mainly because in many states drinking alcoholic beverages is illegal if you're under 21 years of age. Underage drinking can get you into trouble not only with the police, but also with your parents, other teens' parents, and your teachers.

Drinking alcoholic beverages can put both you and your friends in real danger. When you drink—beer, wine, vodka, bourbon, whatever your poison is—alcohol goes into your bloodstream. From there it travels to your central nervous system, which is made up of the spinal cord and brain and controls almost all of your body's functions.

Alcohol blocks messages that are sent to your brain and alters what you see and hear and how you move. It can make you feel and act weird and goofy, slur your speech, and make you stagger and fall down. The polite term for this state is *intoxication,* but let's face it, you're just plain drunk.

A person who is drunk cannot make proper decisions because he cannot think correctly. A drunk cannot drive a car safely and may get into a fight. Teens who drink heavily are more likely to commit suicide. The most common cause of death among teens is car accidents. Almost 40 percent of these accidents are caused by a driver who had been drinking.

Like tobacco, alcohol is extremely addictive. Many people who are alcoholics started drinking when they were quite young. Drinking can destroy your health. Excessive use of alcohol:

✿ Destroys your liver and esophagus and leads to death.

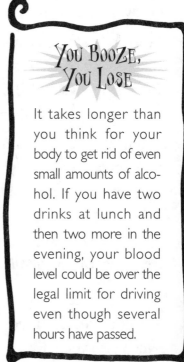

YOU BOOZE, YOU LOSE

It takes longer than you think for your body to get rid of even small amounts of alcohol. If you have two drinks at lunch and then two more in the evening, your blood level could be over the legal limit for driving even though several hours have passed.

❀ Causes high blood pressure, which can lead to heart attack and stroke.

❀ Destroys precious brain cells, causing damage to your brain and nerve function. These cells are *not* replaced by new ones.

❀ Irritates your digestive system, causing ulcers.

❀ Increases your urine output so much that your kidneys may fail.

❀ Can cause impotence (inability to get an erection) in men.

The following suggestions will help you stay alcohol-free:

❀ Choose your friends carefully. It's simple: hang out with guys and girls who do not drink, and you'll avoid being exposed to alcohol.

❀ Don't attend parties where you know booze will be present, or where no adults will be in charge.

❀ When you're with your friends, don't just hang out with nothing to do. Make plans. Go to the mall, see a movie, play sports, go hiking. Having a plan helps you avoid situations where alcohol might be present.

❀ If you do find yourself in a situation where someone is offering you liquor, you can use your parents as an excuse to say no. Many teens find it easier to say, "My parents would KILL me if they knew I was drinking," or "I drank once and got grounded for six months. I'm never going to do it again."

If you'd like more information on alcoholism, or if you have a friend or family member who is—or who you suspect is—alcoholic, turn to the hotlines at the back of this book. You'll find listings for groups and organizations that can help.

DRUGS ARE FOR DUMMIES

Drugs are chemicals. Some can change your body and some your brain. Some are beneficial and are used in medications, such as the antibiotics your doctor gives you when you have a sore throat or an ear infection.

The drugs we are talking about here—the ones for dummies—aren't drugs a doctor would ever give you.

Taking illegal drugs—those available on the street such as heroin, marijuana, cocaine, crack, and methamphetamines (speed)—is never smart, no matter how cool it may seem to you. In fact, people who take drugs don't like to admit they do, even to themselves.

Drugs can cause addiction and death. Even drugs that are prescribed by a doctor can be dangerous IF they are taken by someone other than the person for whom they are prescribed.

Taking drugs can wreak the following havoc on your body and your brain:

❋ Cause depression.

❋ Kill brain cells. Once a brain cell is dead, it's gone forever.

❋ Change the way you think and feel so that you may start believing things are better or worse than they really are.

❋ Cloud your judgment. You may do things you normally wouldn't think of doing.

❋ Damage your liver and other organs you need to lead a healthy life.

❋ Lead to death from an overdose, especially if drugs are taken in combination with alcohol.

❋ Lead to death by suicide.

Teens take drugs for the following reasons:

❋ They want to forget about their problems. However, the drugs work only for a short while. When they wear off, the problem is still there. Drugs don't solve problems; they *cause* problems.

❋ They want to act like adults. Drugs won't make you older—they'll kill you while you're still young.

❋ They want to "fit in."

❋ They are simply curious.

How to Say No—and Make It Stick

It's tough—even scary—to say no when a friend or someone older is encouraging you to try drugs or alcohol. Niki Moyer, M.A., is a psychologist and counselor at Hazelden, the renowned drug and alcohol treatment center in Minnesota. She works with kids and teens who are addicted to drugs and alcohol and trying to kick the habit.

To teach teens how to beat peer pressure and say no with confidence, Moyer uses the following dialogue:

First, ask questions. "What are we going to do over at Bill's house?" If the answer involves smoking, drinking, or doing drugs, by knowing what the plans are, you'll be able to make the right choice.

Then say, "No, thanks." Give a reason or an excuse, such as "I don't smoke."

State the consequences. "If I did that, I'd miss out on going to the movies," or "If I did that, I'd get into trouble."

Suggest another activity. "Why don't we go to the movies?" (or the mall, or the video arcade)

If no one seems interested in doing anything else, walk away. Turn and walk away while you're talking. Your friends will get the idea. If they keep on pressuring you, give them the cold shoulder.

Use a strength-in-numbers strategy whenever possible. This means hanging out with friends who don't use drugs, alcohol, or tobacco, and don't push you to use them either. Choose your friends carefully. You'll benefit from *positive* peer pressure to engage in fun activities rather than dangerous behavior.

LOSSARY

acne: The medical term for pimples, blackheads, whiteheads, skin inflammations, and skin breakouts.

AIDS: The acronym for acquired immune deficiency syndrome. AIDS is a disease caused by the human immunodeficiency virus (HIV). HIV attacks the immune system, which leaves the body less protected against diseases. HIV may not always develop into AIDS in some people, who may live the rest of their lives as HIV-positive. At present there is no cure for AIDS.

alveoli (al-vee-OH-ly): The tiny structures in the breast that produce milk for newborn babies.

ampulla (am-PUHL-uh): The end of the vas deferens, where mature sperm are stored until they are ejaculated.

anorexia nervosa (an-uh-REK-see-uh ner-VOHS-uh): An eating disorder that causes people to starve themselves in order to stay thin.

antibiotics: Medications used to treat diseases or infections caused by bacteria. Antibiotics have no effect on viruses.

areola (ayr-ee-OH-luh): The round, pinkish brown area around the nipple on a breast.

bacterium: A microscopic cell that can cause infection. Bacterial infections are treated with antibiotics.

breast: One of two organs located on the chest wall containing the glands that produce milk for newborn babies. Girls begin developing breasts during puberty.

bulimia (buh-LEEM-ee-uh): An eating disorder that causes people to binge on food, then purge it, which usually involves vomiting or excessive use of laxatives.

calcium: An essential mineral for strengthening bones. Lack of calcium can lead to a condition called osteoporosis, in which bones become brittle and break easily.

cancer: A disease in which abnormal cells grow and divide rapidly, then spread and destroy normal cells.

cervix (SER-viks): The low end of the uterus that joins to the vagina.

circumcision (sur-kum-SIH-zhun): The surgical removal of part or all of the fold of skin covering the glans of the penis.

clitoris (KLIT-uh-rus): The small, knoblike structure in the vulva.

condom: A rubber or latex tube that fits over the penis (or, in the case of the female condom, inside the vagina) to prevent pregnancy or the spread of disease.

Cowper's gland: Located below the prostate, this gland produces some of the fluid that makes up semen. Also called the bulbourethral (bul-boh-yoo-REE-thrul) gland.

dysthymia (dis-THY-mee-uh): A mild form of depression or despondency.

ejaculation (ih-jak-yuh-LAY-shun): The sudden discharge of semen out of the end of the penis at sexual climax.

endometrium (en-doh-MEE-tree-um): The innermost lining of the uterus. During the menstrual cycle, tissue builds up on this lining. If an egg isn't fertilized, the tissue is shed during menstruation. During pregnancy, the endometrium helps to nourish the baby.

endorphins (en-DOR-fins): Chemicals produced in the brain that can improve your mood. Exercise stimulates your body to release endorphins, which is why you feel good after exercising.

enuresis (en-yuh-REE-sis): The uncontrolled or involuntary discharge of urine, commonly called bed-wetting.

epididymis (ep-ih-DID-ih-miss): The long, coiled tube that carries sperm from each testicle. The sperm mature as they pass slowly through the epididymis.

erection: The swelling and hardening of the penis when a male becomes sexually excited, but erections also can happen spontaneously. The swelling is caused by blood flowing into the tissues of the penis.

estrogens: The female sex hormones produced by the ovaries, placenta, and testicles that trigger the female secondary sex characteristics.

fallopian (fuh-LOH-pee-un) **tube**: One of two tubes leading from the top of the uterus, whose opened end is positioned right next to one of the two ovaries. When an egg is released from an ovary, it is swept into a fallopian tube and then into the uterus. Fertilization takes place in the fallopian tube.

fertilization (fert-ul-ih-ZAY-shun): The process in which a male sperm joins with a female egg. Pregnancy begins at fertilization.

genitals: The sexual and reproductive organs. In males, the genitals include the penis, scrotum, and testicles. In females, they include the vagina, uterus, and ovaries.

gonads (GOH-nads): The organs that produce sex hormones. In males, these are the testicles. In females, they are the ovaries.

hormones (HOR-mohnz): A wide variety of protein molecules produced and released from special glands in your body.

hymen (HY-mun): The membranous tissue that partially covers the vaginal opening.

labia majora (LAY-bee-uh muh-JOR-uh): The outer lips of the vulva, outside the vagina.

labia minora (LAY-bee-uh muh-NOR-uh): The lips inside the outer lips that are on either side of the vaginal opening.

lobes (LOHBZ): Several separate milk-producing units that are found in each breast.

menarche (MEN-ar-kee): The onset of menstruation.

menopause (MEN-oh-pawz): The time when menstruation stops, usually between the ages of 45 and 50.

menstrual cycle: The monthly female reproductive cycle.

osteoporosis (AHSS-tee-oh-puh-ROH-sis): A loss of bone volume, usually seen in older women, which results in brittle bones.

ovary (OH-vuh-ree): One of two almond-shaped organs in the female reproductive system. The two ovaries contain all the egg cells needed for reproduction for a lifetime.

ovulation (AHV-yoo-lay-shun): The process in which an egg is released from one of the ovaries and begins to travel to the uterus. Ovulation usually occurs once a month.

ovum (OH-vum): A female's reproductive cell, or egg.

penis: A male's external sexual organ.

pituitary (pih-TOO-eh-ter-ee) **gland**: The structure within the brain that produces several hormones, including follicle-stimulating hormone and luteinizing hormone.

prostate (PRAHSS-tayt): In males, the gland that surrounds the urethra below the bladder. The prostate secretes liquid into the semen.

puberty (PYOO-bur-tee): The physical and emotional changes that take place in everybody between childhood and adulthood.

scrotum (SKROH-tum): The sac of skin that hangs down behind the penis and holds the testicles.

semen (SEE-mun): A liquid made up of sperm and fluids. When a male has an ejaculation, semen comes out of the tip of the penis.

sperm: A male's reproductive cell.

STD: The acronym for sexually transmitted disease. An STD is passed from person to person usually by sexual intercourse or other intimate contact. STDs include genital warts, syphilis, and AIDS.

testicles (TESS-tih-kulz): In a male, the two small egg-shaped organs inside the scrotum that produce sperm.

testosterone (tess-TOSS-tuh-rohn): The male sex hormone produced by the testicles and possibly by the ovaries that triggers the male secondary sex characteristics.

toxic shock syndrome: Also known as TSS, toxic shock syndrome is a disease that has been linked to tampon use. (However, TSS has occurred in men, as well as in women not menstruating.)

urethra (yoo-REE-thruh): The tube leading from the bladder to the outside of the body through which urine passes.

uterus (YOOT-er-us): An upside-down pear-shaped structure inside which a baby grows. The uterus is located in the pelvis.

vagina (vah-JY-nah): The canal that leads from the uterus to the outside of the body. During menstruation, blood and tissue pass through the vagina.

virus (VY-rus): A microscopic organism that reproduces inside living cells. A viral infection is treated with antiviral medications.

vulva (VUL-vah): The genital organs on the outside of the female body.

Hotlines and Referral Agencies

If you or someone you know is in trouble, don't go it alone. Free, confidential help is just a phone call away. Most of these hotlines have toll-free numbers, so there's no reason not to reach out if you know you need help. Here are some hotlines staffed by trained counselors who can provide comfort, referrals to local professionals, and information.

NOTE: In cases of imminent physical trauma, danger, or suicidal behavior, dial 911 or 0 for immediate assistance.

General Assistance

Boys Town of America National Hotline
1-800-448-3000
Provides 24-hour guidance and assistance with all mental and physical health issues related to kids and teens.

Suicide Prevention

Kid Save Hotline
1-800-543-7283
Provides 24-hour crisis intervention and referrals for children and young adults.

National Runaway and Suicide Hotline
1-800-621-4000
Provides 24-hour crisis intervention and assistance for young people who have run away or are considering running away from home.

Sexually Transmitted Diseases

Centers for Disease Control (CDC) National AIDS Hotline
1-800-342-AIDS (342-2437)
Provides 24-hour assistance, referrals, and information related to AIDS and HIV.

CDC National STD Hotline
1-800-227-8922
Questions and concerns answered Mon.–Fri. 8 a.m.–11 p.m. (Eastern Standard Time)

National Herpes Hotline
(919) 361-8488
Questions and concerns answered Mon.–Fri. 9 a.m.–7 p.m. (Eastern Standard Time)

Substance Abuse

Al-Anon and Alateen
1-888-425-2666
A 24-hour hotline for kids and teens who are concerned about a friend or family member's alcohol or drug abuse.

Alcoholics Anonymous (AA)
Call directory assistance for the AA chapter nearest you, or call (212) 870-3400 for referrals and information related to alcoholism.

Center for Substance Abuse Treatment
1-800-662-4357
Provides 24-hour crisis counseling, referrals, and information related to alcoholism and drug use.

Covenant House
1-800-999-9999
Provides 24-hour crisis intervention, assistance, and referrals, especially for young people who have run away or are considering running away from home.

National Hotline for Cocaine Information and Help
1-800-COCAINE (262-2463)
Provides 24-hour help related to cocaine abuse and addiction.

Sexual Assault

Child Help, USA/Child Abuse and Sexual Abuse Hotline
1-800-422-4453
A 24-hour hotline, referral, and information center specializing in child abuse and sexual crimes against children.

Rape, Abuse and Incest Nation Network
1-800-656-4673
A 24-hour hotline that automatically connects you to a counselor near you.

Eating Disorders

The American Anorexia/Bulimia Association
(212) 501-8351
Provides referrals to local eating-disorder therapists, as well as general information.

The National Association of Anorexia Nervosa and Associated Disorders
(847) 831-3438
Provides referrals to local eating-disorder therapists, as well as general information.

Renfrew Eating Disorder Center
1-800-RENFREW (736-3739)
A 24-hour hotline that provides referrals to local eating-disorder treatment centers.

Index

ABOUT THE AUTHOR AND ILLUSTRATORS

Judie Lewellen is the former executive editor of *Shape* magazine. She lives and writes at a small rancho in Littlerock, California, where she also cares for rescued horses, cats, dogs, tortoises, and a dozen species of feathered friends.

Mary Bryson first fell in love with scientific illustration in high school biology class, where she was required to document pig dissections with drawings. She founded Bryson Biomedical Illustrations two years after earning a Master of Associated Medical Sciences in medical illustration. In her studio in Bucks County, Pennsylvania, Mary spends her time chasing her two adorable children, producing art, and laughing with her husband, Jim.

Wendy Wahman's illustrations appear regularly in newspapers, magazines, books, and on greeting cards. You can see more of her work at http://web3.foxinternet.net/caniche.